Product Management Interview Handbook

Aditya Challapally
Edison Tse

www.innovativeinkpublishing.com
Send all inquiries to:
4050 Westmark Drive
Dubuque, IA 52004-1840

Print ISBN: 979-8-3851-1321-7
Ebook ISBN: 979-8-3851-1322-4

Published in the United States of America

Contents

Chapter 2: Analysis of Ideal Answers 17

Chapter 3: Design Fundamentals 45

Chapter 4: Ideal Answers: Product Design.................................75

Preface

Purpose of the Book

It is unfortunate but true: while interviews are intended to assess future job performance, they more often assess a candidate's ability to prepare for interviews. Candidates who know how to prepare properly have distinct advantage.

Adding further complexity, interview preparation does not allow for an iterative testing strategy. It's not practical to test one style of interviewing, then switch to another. Mastering one interview style is challenging enough, and you risk losing valuable job opportunities by testing something ineffective. It is hard to judge which styles or methods are helpful, because intuition, passion, and past experience can point you in the wrong direction.

While researchers have studied interviewing and talent recruiting extensively, they don't have an answer for would-be product managers. Some three decades ago, sociologists started to investigate the mechanism of interviews and interviewers.[1] In 1962, a Harvard researcher published one of the first guides on interview preparation and associated bias in interviews.[2] Unfortunately, research has stayed on this track, focused primarily on biases and improving interview effectiveness for interviewers. Advice for candidates that is backed by formal research, especially for a specific function like product management (product manager), is harder to find.

---

1. Strategies of Effective Interviewing (hbr.org)
2. An Analysis of Precision Learning, Evaluation of Information and Decision-Reaching, in Two Groups, Using Closed Circuit Television (Los Angeles, Western Management Science Foundation, 1962).

To fill the void, an overwhelming number of blogs and articles have been written advising would-be project managers. I read through troves of this content during my own interview preparation process. While well intended, most articles offered sample-size-of-one perspectives, many of which gave blatantly contradictory advice. There was no definitive answer to the burning question: What are interviewers really looking for?

I set out to answer the question for myself. Turning the tables, I interviewed interviewers about interviewing. I started asking friends who were interviewers what they liked to see. With experience across dozens of interviews, they gave answers that were helpful. I thought I could go further.

I emailed over/almost two thousand product management people (product managers) for an even broader sample. About one hundred offered to help. They understood the stress and challenge of interviews. They were also frustrated by the interview process themselves, as you will see in some of the quotes. Interviewing and hiring is draining and time-consuming. It's a big loss for everyone when good candidates are rejected because of an imperfect interview process.

The process is easier and more effective when strong candidates demonstrate the right skills and perform at their best.

I asked these interviewers for three pieces of data:

a)   ideal answers: hiring managers were asked their "ideal" answer to an interviewer question
b)   what wowed them: traits that distinguished candidates as being in the top 5% of applicants they'd interviewed
c)   what put them off: common mistakes candidates make that disqualified them.

I have collected and analyzed this data from about 100 product management interviewers (see Appendix: Survey questions). This book will put you in the interviewer's shoes and look behind the hiring curtain. To paint a rich and rigorous picture of the most successful steps and serious mistakes made by candidates during interviews, this book marries interviewer quotes with unique large-scale analysis.

The advice in this book has been tested and proven in real interviews. I used these insights in my product management interviews. They helped me get a senior title despite interviewing for a junior role. Since then, I've spent over a year mentoring product management candidates through the interview process. They have been overwhelmingly successful. I worked with Professor Edison Tse to improve and streamline the contents to so that it can be complementary to a course on product management. Professor Tse is teaching a course on product management to undergraduate and graduate students at Stanford University. We co-teach a class in the course on manager interview workshop using this material. This is very well received by the students, and we decided to put it out as an interview handbook so that it can be accessible to all those who are interested in perusing a career in product management.

Remember that as you go through this, we are all rooting for you! The world needs better products and more people to make them.

Aditya Challanpally

Book Setup

People have found that the Analysis of Ideal Answers and Design Fundamentals to be particularly useful, while the ideal answers is used as more of a reference.

Below is a more in-depth explanation of each section.

1. **High-level traits**
   Chapter structure:
   - Type of questions
   - What wows interviewers
   - What puts off interviewers
   - Approach
   - Other: ideas/commentary/etc.

2. **Analysis of Ideal Answers**
   Description: This is an analysis of the ideal answers for all the major types of questions, with quotes and statistics backing almost every insight. It also contains the rough frameworks that all the ideal answers used.

   Aim: This section aims to explain what interviewers want to hear for each question (e.g., 9/10 said that they liked to hear this) based off the surveys and ideal answers. ~100% of the product managers hated using frameworks, but ironically all followed similar structures for each question. Note that each product manager stuck a structure only to a point that it helped them make their answers clear and linear. You are unique and have unique experiences, so work to highlight them and bring your creative ideas and unique perspective to the interview.

Chapter structure:
- Type of questions
- What wows interviewers
- What puts off interviewers
- Approach
- Other: ideas/commentary/etc.

3. **Design Fundamentals**

Description: Design Fundamentals dives into the fundamental pieces (e.g., user selection, goal selection, problem selection) that came up in all questions. We will apply these principles to an example done by an Amazon principal product manager for "How would you improve Alexa to increase usage?"

Aim: Mastering these fundamentals will help you in behavioral, product design, product strategy, and analytical questions.

Chapter structure:
- What wows interviewers
- What puts off interviewers
- Approach
- Applying to improve the Alexa problem
- Other: interesting ideas/etc.

4. **Ideal Answers**

Description: Of the 71 answers, 7 are cleaned up and transcribed in this book. There is a selection of both "bad" and "good" ideal answers (some hiring managers didn't have the greatest responses). Along with detailed answers, product managers provided comments about where their mock candidates/people typically fail as well as the best answers they have heard for their questions.

Aim: For you to reference after you have tried the question.

Chapter structure:
- Interviewer thoughts
- Answer
- My thoughts

Feel free to use this book as a step-by-step guide or as a reference. Happy trails!

Practicing

APPROACH

It is common to see people prepping to do 30+ mock interviews with friends or product managers. This works for some, but it is not the most efficient use of time, nor the most effective for developing good interview skills. It is more important to practice mindfully. Product manager interviewers generally recommend some version of these steps, which ends up being about 10 mock interviews with other people:

1. Start with 2–3 practice mocks to understand how an interview is done.
2. Do five self-mocks (see section How to do self-mocks).
3. Read best practice answers for those five questions (optional).
4. Create and add to your user pain points and ideas list.
5. Do one practice mock with an experienced product managers (or self-mocks if you don't have access to an experienced product manager, someone who has done at least 2–3 product manager mocks already).
6. Repeat Steps 2–5 about 5 times to get good and 9–10 times to get really good.

The most valuable step is probably Step 4, in which you compile high-level pain points and interesting ideas. Maintaining an ongoing list will foster creativity, help you generate ideas in an interview setting, and give you a large repertoire of ideas to quickly pull from in an interview setting. The key takeaway—it is more important to do fewer mocks and learn from them than to just factory-pump through them.

How to do self-mocks

Product managers give themselves "self-mocks" on a daily or weekly basis. It's how we do our jobs! Self-mocks will help you 10 times more than just doing mocks with other folks. Unlike mocks with another person, where a key goal is to simulate the pressure of an interview setting, self-mocks provide ample time to pause and reflect.

Too many people start with the "mock interview" without figuring out the basics. It is hard to come up with novel insights when you are stressed in a 15-minute interview mock. Emphasize self-mocks more than practice mocks.

How to do it:

1. Pick a question that has a sample answer that you can compare to and, if using this book, read the "What Interviewer Looks For" and "Common Mistakes" sections.
2. Write out your answer on a piece of paper or computer.
3. Read the sample answer.
4. Compare and reflect (use the analysis provided but also think of your own analysis).
5. Once you feel confident with written answers, move on to voicing your thoughts out loud.
6. For parts of the mock that would require interviewer interaction, experiment with different reactions.

In daily life

It can be helpful to incorporate product insight practice into your daily life. It adds variety and lets you think through problems with real-world context. For example, you can:

- Go look at products and justify why people made certain decisions.
- Criticize coffee makers and backpacks and other normal items and brainstorm improvements.
- Read news about product releases or changes.

PLANNING YOUR PREPARATION

Candidates often make one of two common preparation mistakes: they either (i) spend too much time on preparation and delay applying or (ii) apply immediately and then have far too little time to prepare. dom. If there is truly only one thing, recommend "Both of these mistakes are driven by the same root cause. It's difficult to judge the amount of time it will take to fully prepare.

There is no rule or approach to determine the exact length of preparation time needed. It depends on your background and current skill level. However, from my experience mentoring candidates, it is much more common for candidates to overestimate the time required, especially, the more eager ones. They think they need to do 30+ interview mocks to improve their chances. In my anecdotal experience, with mindful practice and a focus on self-mocks, a good performance level can be reached in about 20 days of focused work. Again, this is an anecdotal value. Plan and think through what you need to do to get comfortable.

High-Level Traits

It is difficult to determine patterns for medium-sized companies with statistical certainty. It seems to be a mix between startups and large companies. Interviewers start to ask different questions and prefer different answers as the size of the company increases. The interviewers from smaller medium-sized companies still seem to act like startup product managers. Accordingly, the interviewers from larger medium-sized companies seem to act like large company product managers.

Job of a Product Manager

The main objective of a product manager is to create business impact. Releasing features, solving bugs, creating new products for customers, discussing technical architecture, and other responsibilities are the tools a product manager uses to accomplish this.

Product managers are at the intersection of design, marketing/sales/business, and engineering. They work with colleagues from each of these functions to build a product. Product managers have no authority over any of these functions. They don't have the option to just give orders. Instead, they have to influence and convince stakeholders to provide resources.

As such, product managers need to have the skills and knowledge to communicate with and influence design, engineering, and business folks. For business folks, it is important to be familiar with strategic/analytical skills. For design folks, it's user empathy and design skills. For engineering, it's technical knowledge. It is important that product managers are proficient in these skills not just to influence and understand, but to bring insights. The best product managers bring their unique perspective to discussions with other functions, rather than just listening and accepting advice.

It is important to acknowledge that there are various types of product managers (e.g., growth, technical). The importance of each of the product management skills varies across different role specializations and companies. Different companies also have different engineering and product cultures, which translates to different flavors of product management. While nuances matter, there are common threads across all flavors of product management that form the core of the profession.

In summary, the skills that product managers use regularly are, in no particular order:

- Technical knowledge
- Collaboration/leadership skills
- Communication skills
- Strategic/analytical skills
- Design skills
- Deep user empathy

Interviewers ask questions to judge your proficiency in these six skills.

Hiring Process Overview

This section outlines the typical steps in the product management hiring process and highlights the key types of questions candidates face in interviews. Before getting into the details, an important thing to keep in mind: the interviewer wants you to succeed. They are rooting for you. In fact, some of them might even be desperate for you to succeed since hiring takes a lot of time and energy. They are taking 0.5–1 hour out of their day to interview you. They would have rejected you earlier if they wanted you to fail. Keep this in mind when you're feeling nervous or if you think the interviewer is cold.

PROCESS

The process is laid out below. Recruiters and hiring managers from various companies were asked about the typical pass rate for each stage.

- Resume selection (~2% pass rate)
- Recruiter screen (pass rate not applicable)
- Initial round, usually two 0.5–1-hour interviews (~%10 pass rate)
- Take-home assignment, mostly for startups (pass rate not applicable)
- Final round, usually four 0.5–1-hour interviews (~40% pass rate)
- Negotiation and offer

QUESTIONS

There are four types of questions you are generally asked in a product manager interview, listed below. Large and small companies tend to focus on different question types

- Product Design (e.g., design an alarm clock for the blind)
- Product Strategy (e.g., should Google acquire Netflix?)
- Analytical, metric/goal based (e.g., you are a product manager on FB News Feed; what metrics would you track for success?), classic estimation question (e.g., how much does Gmail pay for storage annually?), and bug based (e.g., all of Google Malaysia is down; what happened?)
- Technical, usually rare (e.g., sorting, linked lists, arrays, strings)

Refer to the section Questions by company size analysis to understand what types of questions big companies ask.

Refer to the section on Analysis of Ideal Answers to understand how to answer these questions.

Paths to Product Manager and Associated Success Rates

The ideal way to determine the best path to become a product manager would be to look at current product managers and analyze their paths. Specifically, we would analyze the jobs and activities they did before becoming a product manager. Fortunately, this is a picture we can put together with LinkedIn pages of product managers. Below is a breakdown of the position approximately 2,000 people had before their first product management job.

CURRENT
COMPOSITION (%)

Business externally*	7%
College student	8%
Engineering or design**	24%
MBA student	27%
Business internally*	35%

The least common path for a product manager is external business applicants (7%). The most common background for a product manager is through an internal transfer from a business job (35%). About 1/4 of product managers are straight from MBA.

We can find this by asking hiring managers for the breakdown of applicants they see for junior/mid-level product management openings (e.g., usually 10% of applicants are MBA students). We can then divide the breakdown of product manager applicants by the current composition of product managers. With this approximation, we can get to a "Success Index" per path. Below is the Success Index for all the paths, sourced from asking approximately 30 hiring managers.

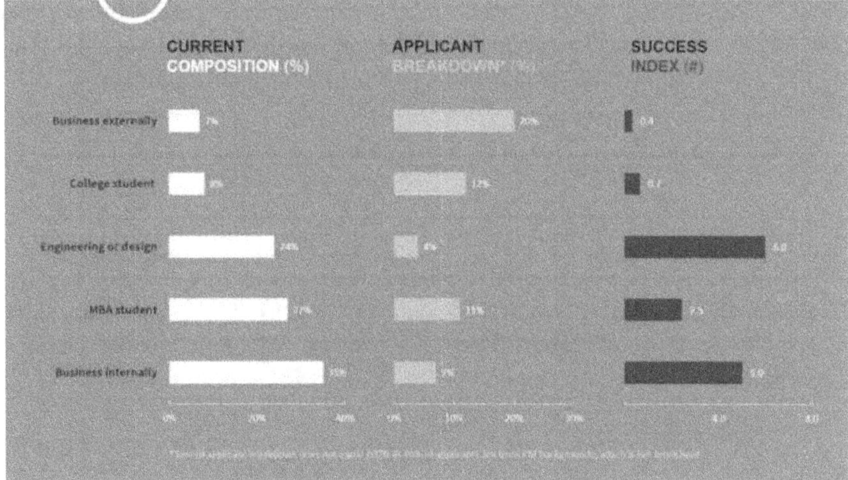

A shocking 54% of people that apply to junior/mid-level product management jobs have no previous product management experience, as only 46% apply with previous product manager experience. The least successful path is to apply directly from an external business job (0.4). The most successful path for an applicant without an engineering/design background is through an internal transfer (5.0). For a non-technical person, the best chance they must enter product management is through an internal transfer.

OVERALL TAKEAWAYS FOR APPLYING TO PRODUCT MANAGER

For a non-technical (e.g., not engineering) candidate, the best chance for you to enter product management is through an internal transfer (e.g., already inside the company).

Replicate the ease that MBA programs offer to hiring managers to find good candidates by getting a referral. Do not send a cold email as they really, really do not like cold emails.

Be extremely selective about your product-adjacent role as the specific job can significantly increase or decrease your chances of getting into product management.

Focus on developing unique subject matter experience (e.g., insurance processes for Fintech company, drop shipping for e-commerce companies) if you are in a non-technical role, especially if you are an external candidate.

To answer the above question, we asked approximately 30 hiring managers to rank the importance of certain traits on a scale of 1–10. Below is the average for each trait.

Every hiring manager indicated previous product manager experience as extremely important (10). Unique subject matter experience is almost as highly valued as previous engineering experience (~8). Having an MBA does not matter much to hiring managers (2).

There are three paths that we should explore more deeply: a) MBA, b) internal transfer, and c) external applicants.

A. MBA

There is a discrepancy between the high success rate of the MBA path and the low importance of having a "MBA."

Hiring is a strenuous and time-sucking process. MBA programs do a really great job of structuring recruiting opportunities for large companies. So, while hiring managers do not really care about candidates having an MBA, they are more inclined to accept candidates that have been directly funneled to them. This large discrepancy clearly shows the value of this recruiting process.

If you can replicate the ease at which hiring managers can find and hire you (not just applying online), you can replicate part of the hiring value for an MBA program.

B. INTERNAL TRANSFERS

The success rate for the internal transfer is high because "previously worked with person," and "unique subject matter experience" are valued. Most importantly, the folks in product-adjacent roles that develop "unique subject matter expertise" are more successful in transitioning to product management. Unique subject matter expertise allows product-adjacent folks to differentiate themselves against candidates with product manager experience.

There are two extremely common mistakes people make when selecting or doing these product-adjacent roles:

i) They pick roles or niches that do not allow them to build unique subject matter experience. To select the best product-adjacent role, it helps to ascertain exactly how much exposure you get to product decisions (e.g., "How often do you push back against product decisions?").

ii) They think that just doing their job extremely well qualifies them to get a product management role. While it is very important to do well in your role, hiring managers won't hire you because of your expertise in your own field (e.g., communications), they will hire you because of your subject matter experience.

Be extremely selective about your product-adjacent role as it can significantly increase your chances of getting into product management.

C. EXTERNAL APPLICANTS

If you are an external non-technical candidate (e.g., consultant), develop unique subject matter expertise to increase your chances of getting into product management directly. The bar for unique subject matter expertise is even higher for external candidates than for internal candidates. The product managers straight from external business roles (7%) were almost exclusively highly specialized consultants (e.g., procurement consultants working for supply chain startups, payroll consultants working for HRTech startups).

This does not necessarily work for popular areas (e.g., e-commerce, social media, ads), where there are hundreds of thousands of people, and thousands of product managers, that have subject matter expertise. It is much more difficult to transition to product management roles in these areas from a non-technical role. Focus on developing unique subject matter experience if you are in a non-technical role, especially if you are an external candidate.

What Interviewers Value in Interviews

Interviewers value traits that match up with the skills that product managers need. They ask specific questions to test specific skills. For example, they will ask product design questions to test design skill, user empathy, and communication skills.

- Technical knowledge
- Collaboration/leadership skills
- Communication skills
- Strategic thinking
- Design skills
- Deep user empathy.

The importance of each of these skills varies by the type of job and the type of company, so it was difficult to find a consensus for the prioritization of the "hard" skills (e.g., technical knowledge, design skills, strategic thinking). We will dig into the importance of these "hard" skills later in Questions by company size Analysis of Ideal Answers. Product manager interviewers were asked to rate the following traits in terms of importance from 1 to 10 for the overall interview:

Empathy, Creativity, Clarity, Speed, and Personable (e.g., Likability). Almost all interviews provided the exact same answer for this prioritization exercise.

RESULTS FROM SURVEY

Clarity is the most valued

A significant part of interview prep material and our own intuition tells us that it is more important to prioritize content over delivery. Most of the candidates focus most of their preparation on content while leaving only the last 10% on delivery. However, the survey data indicates that interviewers consistently prioritize clarity to be the most valued (~10/10). If you want to get better at interviews, perfecting your delivery will significantly increase your performance. If you are clear, concise, and confident instead of wordy, nervous, and digressive, you're going to be at the top of the hiring list. Research indicates that high self-confidence correlates with significantly better delivery and better interview performance.[1]

A product manager's job is to communicate with and influence stakeholders. The content of those discussions will vary significantly, from product design decisions to customer complaints. The interviewer is foremost judging your ability to act under pressure and communicate effectively. Therefore, a stressful interview creates the perfect environment to judge your ability to perform a significant part of the job.

Finding someone who can communicate clearly and succinctly in this stressful setting is rare. As one Amazon Sr. Manager, product manager explained:

> *It's honestly so rare to find a person that speaks clearly. I want to feel like I am having a chat with a product colleague. It's a terrible meeting if they just ramble for 20 minutes.*

Creativity is the least valued

It is important that you come up with compelling solutions during the interview. However, compelling solutions come from finding burning problems and solving the problem effectively, not by thinking of creative new ways of

---

1. https://www.researchgate.net/publication/340020160_Applicant%27s_Self_Confidence_Influence_in_Employment_Interview_Process_According_to_Recruiters_Perceptions_An_Exploratory_Study_in_Greece

solving a problem. It is not necessary to create extremely fringe or wildly aggressive solutions. Product manager hiring managers valued creativity the least (5/10). As one Facebook product manager explained:

> *I've done more than 300 interviews now. I have heard everything at this point. I am not looking for someone to wow me with a crazy VR/AR/mind-link idea. I want to see clarity of thought and a compelling solution. The best solutions do not have to be the most creative, they must solve the problem that you laid out earlier in the interview. That itself is a rare find!*

Empathy is rare

Clarity was rated higher than empathy, but empathy was still highly valued and was the second most valuable trait. Interviews mentioned that it was still quite rare to find candidates with deep user empathy. Most candidates have empathy, but they struggle to show it in their interviews. A really easy way to show empathy is thinking about the details of your solution, which we will walk through later in Design Fundamentals. One Dropbox Director, Product discussed the prioritization between clarity and empathy:

> *I would prioritize this over clarity, as empathy is the most important aspect for a product manager, but really good clarity is so rare that I gave it a 10. I am sure I've interviewed a bunch of candidates who had really good empathy, but I couldn't follow their logic. Having empathy is important but being able to demonstrate empathy is even more important.*

Being happy is a differentiator

It is natural to feel nervous and stressed during an interview. But being happy and relaxed makes you more personable to the interviewer. Interviewers rated the importance of being personal as 7/10. As one former Google Gproduct manager and current VP Product of a Series C startup mentioned:

> *I'll like a candidate more if they are excited and happy. I go to 8 back-to-back meetings with serious topics and serious people. If I must spend 30 minutes with a serious or super nervous person during an interview, that is fine, I will still pass them if they do well. But if they are confident and happy, it is a lot easier to listen to what they have to say and I am happier to work with them.*

In summary, energy, clarity, and empathy are the most important traits to demonstrate in a product management interview.

The simplified results for the entire survey are below:

- Clarity: 10
- Empathy: 8
- Personable: 6
- Speed: 5
- Creativity: 5

APPROACH

To incorporate the above insights, use the following approach before and during the interview:

a. Before the interview, read the chapter on Delivery patterns and focus more of your effort on delivery. Record yourself doing self-mocks and check if you are being clear.
b. Take time to think before speaking, and do not worry about taking too long. Interviewers valued speed as the least important trait in the interview.
c. Do not worry about the pressure to come up with creative ideas. Focus on solving the problem as effectively as possible.
d. Enjoy the process, as it will make you happier and make you seem more relaxed.

What Startup Interviewers Value

This chapter dives into the preferences of interviewers at startups.

There are three parts to the analysis: a. Question distribution, b. What wows interviewers, c. Key tips.

A. QUESTION DISTRIBUTION

Below is breakdown and frequency of the types of questions that startup interviewers asked:

- 60% product design (e.g., "improve our product")
- 20% behavioral (e.g., "how do you deal with a frustrated dev?")
- 10% strategy (e.g., "what do you think we should sell next?")
- <5% analytical (e.g., estimation, goal-setting, metric diagnostic)
- <5% technical (e.g., "how would you design an API for our product?")

Startup interviewers focused much more on product design and culture fit rather than strategy, analytical, and technical questions. Specifically in product design, questions were generally around execution more that high-level strategy.

Their questions were also a lot more associated with their own product. Almost 70% of the questions they said they commonly asked were related to their specific industry. For example, it is rare for them to ask general questions like "design a backpack" but much more common to ask specific questions like "improve [our product] for [example user]." If they were to ask a generic question, it is more likely that they would ask about your favorite product. To prepare for that question, read the chapter on Favorite product answer patterns.

They also consistently had take-home assignments. About 70% of startup and high-growth companies had a take-home assignment. Almost 100% of the assignments were associated with the company or the company's product.

B. WHAT WOWS INTERVIEWERS

Practical, solid ideas

In the analysis of all the interview answers, **almost no startup product manager (~0%) had answers with crazy/moonshot ideas**. Some product managers mentioned that it can be refreshing to see crazy/moonshot ideas from candidates but not necessary. Some of them considered to be a waste of time to consider them.

Focus on solution design and risks

Ideal answers from startup product managers were a lot more focused around solution design and risks, not as much on problem definition and customer/use case brainstorming. We'll be explaining these steps in more detail in the section on Analysis of Ideal Answers. Their ideal answers had more than 1/2 of the time spent on solution UI/UX Design and associated launch/build/testing planning. They prize execution over idea generation and want product managers to be able to hit the ground running.

Practical steps

They really appreciated answers that included practical steps in being a product manager, especially when designing the solution. Product manager interviewers said, "Writing a PRD", "Speaking with engineering lead", etc. were all phrases that they looked for. About 20% of startup product managers asked candidates to write user stories during every interview to test specific dev or design experience.

Alignment with goal

About 90% of startup product managers mentioned that they wanted the candidate to **consider alignment with company goals when choosing a problem**. As one VP Product of a Series B startup explained:

> *Say you are improving an e-commerce checkout product for a startup that wants to focus on creating a global brand. If you were choosing between two problems like 'our checkout payments process is extremely confusing' or 'the UI of our product does not work well in international cultures', even though the first problem may be more compelling, I appreciate it more when the candidate picks the UI problem because it aligns with our company's goals.*

C. KEY TIPS

1. Before the interview, understand the company's current situation, its challenges, and industry.
2. Before the interview, brainstorm and/or understand their users in detail.
3. Leave at least half the time for solution design in your answers.
4. Consider resource constraints in your answers constantly to make your solutions practical, unless explicitly asked not to. An example to illustrate the point:

   > *If a company only raised $1M and only has 50 business customers, proposing advanced analytics and AI as a solution would not be practical. They do not have the scale to have complicated data storage systems and do not have the money to invest in machine training.*

5. At the end of the interview, when testing the success of the product, keep your answers less focused on using or finding "data" to back up assump-

tions, but much more around iterating fast and finding and speaking with customers. An example from the ideal answers:

> *Ideally, after launch, we would start tracking success metrics right away in terms of usage, but I am not sure if that'll be helpful at this point since we won't have that much data. Because it is a relatively new product, I would like to talk to new adopters and ask them about their behavior to judge success and discover further iterations.*

6. Learn how epics and stories are written. About 70% of startup product manager interviewers ask specific execution details in their interviews.

What Large Company Interviewers Value

A. QUESTION DISTRIBUTION

This is a generalization based off survey results and varies significantly by company (e.g., Amazon focuses almost 100% on behavioral).

- 50% product design (e.g., "design a better backpack")
- 20% strategy (e.g., "do you think we should buy [competitor]?")
- 10% analytical (e.g., "our metrics are down, what happened?")
- 10% behavioral (e.g., "what was a time you had a disagreement with your engineering manager?")
- 5% technical (e.g., "how does Google Docs work?")
- 5% other (e.g., "launch Microsoft Stream in Australia").

While there was still a focus on product design, interviews at large companies have more of an emphasis on strategy and analytical skills compared to interviews at startups. Interviews at large companies also have less focus on behavioral questions than interviews at startups. The notable exception is Amazon where almost 100% of the questions are behavioral.

In addition, very few questions at large companies are associated with the company's product. Instead, interviewers at large companies asked questions about everyday items and general products. A few examples from the ideal answers:

> *"Design a better video sharing site", "Design a better airport experience", "What is your favorite product?", etc.*

In addition, almost none have taken home assignments. It sometimes varied between the department and job, but almost 0% had any take-home assignment.

B. WHAT WOWS INTERVIEWERS

Ambitious and bold ideas

Large companies have resources, capital, and networks and they want to know that product managers can use all available resources to create an amazing future. Almost every product manager (90%) of a large company had crazy/moonshot ideas in their ideal answers.

However, do not focus solely on pushing creative ideas for the sake of having a crazy/moonshot idea. It is still important to solve the actual problem effectively. The takeaway here is that interviewers at large companies value crazy/moonshot ideas more in an interview setting than interviewers at startups.

Focus on user and problem selection

Where interviewers from startups were more focused on designing a viable solution with an effective go-to-market plan, interviewers from large companies were more focused on testing the candidate's ability to find the most compelling problem and user. In their ideal answers, interviewers from large companies spent more than ½ the time just on picking a user and a problem. This is much higher than interviewers from startups, who spent less than 1/3 the time on these two components, instead spending much more time on solution design, execution, and go-to-market planning.

Emphasis on user delight

In their ideal answers, product managers from large companies constantly used and emphasized creating delightful experiences for users, regardless of cost or development time. Startup product managers were more focused on products that were relatively fast and cheap to build so that they could quickly iterate on the product.

This logic makes sense especially when you compare the circumstances and consumer expectations of large companies against startups. If a large company, like Apple, launched an extremely cheaply built product, it would lose customer trust. If a startup launched the same product, because of lower consumer expectations, it wouldn't lose the same amount of customer trust.

In ideal answers of large company interviewers, they used these phrases whenever they referred to creating a well-built product:

> *"Delighting user," "Fun for user," "gamification," "seamless user experience"*

Data and metrics

Large companies have millions of users and great telemetry to track that usage. product managers who work at these companies work with data on a daily basis. Almost every single answer (100%) from large company product managers included a section for metrics to track success. They also mentioned that they were impressed when a candidate demonstrated a clear strong grasp of data and metrics. Product managers were particularly impressed if a candidate mentioned how they would use data to identify problems. Here is an example from an ideal answer by a Google product manager director:

> *After launch, I would look at three major metrics to track usage: a) downloads in first 30 days, b) attrition in the first 90 days, and c) daily active users for the next 120. Given that we want to see fast success from this, I've given noticeably short timelines and I am mostly tracking users rather than specific behavior or purchases as our goal was just around increased usage.*

C. KEY TIPS

1. Before the interview, spend some time to learn about the company and its users but unlike prepping for startups, spend more time on your general fundamentals and user empathy skills.
2. Make your answers bold, ambitious, and creative.
3. Do not consider resource constraints in answers, unless explicitly asked to.
4. Spend at least ½ the time to make sure you nail the right problem and show clear user empathy.
5. At the end, explain how you would use data to test success and validate all assumptions.

Analysis of Ideal Answers

Introduction

<u>Aim:</u> This section aims to explain what interviewers are looking for when they ask a question (e.g., 9/10 said that they liked to hear this) based off the surveys and ideal answers.

<u>Description:</u> In these chapters, we describe each of the common product management interview questions in detail. More importantly, we discuss what types of answers interview managers do and do not like using statistics and interview quotes.

In addition to analyzing their survey and interview responses, we also analyzed their ideal answers to find the rough framework they used for each type of question. While not all of them followed the structure, each product manager used some of the framework to make their answers clear and linear.

As you go through the frameworks, remember to use them mindfully. You are unique and have unique experiences, so work to highlight them and bring your creative ideas and unique perspective to the interview.

Each chapter has the following structure:

- Types of questions
- What wows interviewers
- What puts off interviewers
- Approach (how should you approach preparation and the interview)
- Other: Ideas/Commentary/etc.

Chapters:

- Behavioral answer patterns
- Product design answer patterns
- Strategy answer patterns
- Analytical answer patterns
- Favorite product answer patterns
- Other question patterns

Behavioral Answer Patterns

TYPE OF QUESTIONS

There are over 100+ behavioral questions that product manager interviewers ask (view Appendix: Example behavioral questions). From the survey that interviewers filled out, there about five types of questions that consistently showed up. The frequency of each type of question is shown below (e.g., 90% means that on average, interviewers ask it in 90% of interviews).

- Tell me about yourself—100%
- Tell me about "X" experience from resume with follow-up questions on challenges—90%
- Instance where you persuaded someone (e.g., engineer, designer) to adopt an agenda that they initially resisted—70%
- Instance where you effectively managed a difficult stakeholder (e.g., customer, manager)—50%
- Instance where you led people to achieve a nearly unachievable goal—30%

WHAT WOWS INTERVIEWERS

In general, interviewers ask behavioral questions to test the following traits: clarity, empathy, culture fit, impact, leadership experience, and teamwork. In the survey, we asked interviewers to rank the importance of these traits on a scale of 1–10. Each of these traits were defined so that there would be no ambiguity (e.g. impact referred to the tangible/financial effect of the candidate's actions.)

These are the results from the survey:

- Empathy: 10
- Clarity: 9
- Culture fit: 8
- Impact: 8
- Teamwork: 5
- Leadership experience: 5

Leadership and impact is not an absolute priority

Leadership was ranked the least important and impact was also not highly ranked. This is very counterintuitive and quite shocking, considering the job of a product manager is to create impact. The common consensus among interviewers was that while leadership and impact were quite important, the other traits were even more important. While a product manager needs to have impact, achieving that impact with empathy and in a manner that matches with the company's culture was critical. One Amazon Sr. product manager elaborated:

> *Leadership and impact are critical to a product manager's job. But fitting into our culture and having boat loads of clear empathy matter way more. If they show culture fit and clear examples of empathy, they will naturally be a great leader and team player in our culture. I'd rather someone told me about a time they weren't in a leadership position and accomplished something impressive through influence and empathy.*

We have covered the inherent lack of authority of a product manager in previous chapters. They only gain authority through influence and trust so the emphasis on empathy and culture fit is logical. One Facebook product manager said:

> *Trust is a greater force than control. You get control indirectly via trust. If a person just prioritizes just impact, I won't be hiring them.*

Engaging storytelling

Interviewers are looking for a powerful and clear story, not just a regurgitation of your resume. According to the interviewers, only about ~10% of candidates craft an engaging story.

Interviewers listen to hundreds of candidates with similar behavioral stories around bad bosses, difficult customers, and tough projects. Therefore, it can be difficult to differentiate yourself purely with the content of your story. It is easier to differentiate yourself and engage the interview by improving the format and delivery of your story. One Amazon Sr. Manager, Product explained:

> *The best stories are when I am hooked, and it is bit like a great TV show. There is a little bit of drama, a little bit of suspense, big impact, and big splashes. And the candidate emerges as the hero. How could I not pass that person? They just made a movie featuring their own lives.*

Apart from a more compelling narrative, an additional way to engage the interviewer is to actively include the interview in the discussion. Check in with the interviewer to make sure they are following along and ask them about their thoughts. One example is to offer options to the interviewer so that they can choose which parts of your story they want to explore. ~60% of candidates do not usually even check in during the entire behavioral section. An Amazon principal product manager provided some stats to illustrate:

> *I like it when people check in because it allows me to direct the story, if I choose to, kind of like an interactive movie. 50% of the time I just tell the candidate to continue, but sometimes I'll redirect and ask a few questions and those detours are always the interesting parts.*

Even when crafting a creative story, make sure that you prioritize being clear and concise. Also be very selective about the words and phrases you use to craft your story. For example, using the phrase "put myself in their shoes" or the word "empathize" in your story can help highlight your empathy to the interview.

In the Approach section, we will walk through some tips for effective storytelling.

WHAT PUTS OFF INTERVIEWERS

Rambling

Interviewers rated clarity to be the most important trait to demonstrate in the overall interview and the second most important trait to demonstrate in the behavioral section.

Keep your stories short and allow for interviewers to probe more. It is extremely difficult for an interviewer to interrupt you. So even if you start rambling, they can't help you stop. Not one interviewer complained that candidates explained too little in their behavior. Also, by explaining too much upfront, you do not build enough suspense in your story and probably bore the interviewer. A Facebook product manager said:

> *Next time I have to listen to another behavioral story where a candidate starts reading off their resume or starts throwing big words at me, I think I am going to just interrupt them... Actually, I don't interrupt somebody because that is a terrible candidate experience. But I feel like doing it so often.*

Not getting the interview excited upfront

Imagine going to the movie theatre and then getting pushed into a random screening for a movie that you have never seen the trailer for and are not familiar with at all. For most of the movie, you'd probably be confused and unhappy. Most people would hate to get pushed around like that.

But candidates do this to interviewers quite frequently in interviews. Candidates dive right into their story without setting the context or getting the interviewer excited. Excite the interviewer upfront by answering one question: why does this story matter?

Lead with impact of the story to get the interviewer engaged and excited, and then talk about your actions.

As much as the interviewer is judging your actions for empathy and culture fit, your story becomes exciting when it has a large impact. For example, say you solved a tough challenge with a customer with great empathy and deep trust. That is wonderful to hear, but why did it matter? Who cares if the customer left? Were they a big customer? Did they give you more sales after you solved the problem?

Tease some of these points at the beginning of your story so that the interviewer is excited and engaged.

Media companies create headlines to get people to come listen to their story, like a trailer for a movie or a great tagline for a book. Create a headline for your story. We will explore this in the headline point of the Using HCARL section in this chapter.

APPROACH

Interviewers are not looking for frameworks. They are looking for one thing: **a compelling story where you emerge as the compassionate and ultimate hero.** Follow the steps laid out in this Approach to create that story:

1. Follow a framework that has some form of the following: **Headline, Context, Action, Results, Learning (see Using HCARL section later in this chapter).**

2. **Use phrases that show clear empathy**. It is important to highlight the moments that you showed empathy.

   The first step I took was to put myself in Matt's shoes," "brought him along for the ride, "put it in his language.

3. **Add more detail** to the experience to turn it into a real story (e.g., who said what in conversation, what did that look like?)

   They were saying ___. And I interpreted it as ___ based on the context of ___. And then I took this action.

   When I told our customer that we had to delay the release again, I saw his face start to redden and his jaw clench and a yell bubbling up, and I knew that if he started yelling, this meeting wouldn't be productive. So, I immediately handed it off to his colleague that I'd already briefed on the issue so she could calm him down.

4. **Put in cliff-hangers** at the end of each section and ask if they are following. Ideally, you make it so exciting that they ask, "so what did you do from there?!"

5. **Pick an experience that had a large impact**. While impact does not matter as much to interviewers as much as empathy and clarity, the story is a lot more engaging if it's a high-stakes experience. Pick a story with important people, a tight deadline, and an impossible task. If you don't have an experience like this, read Context in Using HCARL to frame your experiences in this light.

6. **Put names to people**, especially the main antagonist. If you have a troubling customer, name them "Chris" or "Zach" rather than constantly referring to them as "the customer." Again, it helps paint the experience in a more tangible light for the interview.

7. **Keep stats at minimum.** Use statistics to show the magnitude of impact/problem, but use quotes to deepen the story. Using too many numbers can be confusing. Prioritize using a customer's or colleague's sentiment to showcase your empathy. Here's an example that combines stats and sentiment:

> *We implemented a product for factory workers that would save the company $1M per year. What stuck with me is that at the end of summer, a union worker said 'Alex, we are really going to miss you, nobody has ever treated us like people before.' More than the financial impact, that's what convinced them to use our product.*

Using HCARL

Using this framework will ensure you create a compelling story:

- **Headline.** Use two sentences to summarize the story that grabs their attention, much like an article headline or a movie trailer. Ensure that you showcase your impact, not your actions. Once you pitch the headline, ask the interviewer if that is something they would want to hear. For an even more engaging experience, provide two headlines and ask the interview which one they want to hear—forcing them to engage even more.

  > *Not: "I created an accounting product for CPAs at XBank that was really difficult to build because of customer demands, various regulatory hurdles, and other time commitments when I was an intern".*

  > *Instead: "I thought of and built a product as an intern that completely changed the way CPAs at XBank did a ¼ of their job."*

- **Context.** Setup the context to make the task seem like an insurmountable challenge.

  > *When I pitched the idea to my intern manager, he did not trust that it was possible at all, vehemently rejected it, and brushed me off like one other intern wasting his time and told me not to bring it up again. When I went to 5 other managers, they also rejected me.*

- **Action.** Do not just start talking about your actions. Choose the three most important actions you did and phrase each with a mini justification. Use empathy and data as much as possible to justify your actions. For example, when you are trying to convince people, you could use the following three steps: 1. Understand their reasoning 2. Gather data to counter reasoning 3. Use empathy to frame your next pitch in their language/mindset to convince them of your reasoning.

  > Not: *"To solve this problem, I immediately started messaging people to see if they would support me in my pitch."*

  > Instead: *"I looked at it from his perspective and thought about all the interns he must have had and how he must basically looking to minimize risk and saw that he didn't trust software and more importantly, he didn't trust me just yet. So, instead of searching for ROI data, I went and searched for data to show that the risk was minimal. Then I set out to do the following three things."*

- **Result.** Slow down near the end so that you build up to the climax. Phrase your impact in the most favorable lens. For example, if revenue from the product is low, potentially frame your impact around user growth.

  > *After my presentation, now it was up to my boss to decide. For about two minutes of sullen silence, we just sat across from each other. He finally said 'okay, you've proven it is minimal risk, so let's do a full-scale pilot.' We did it in 2 months and created $100k in savings.*

Product Design Answer Patterns

Product design questions are quite common because they test almost all the traits that a product manager needs (e.g., clarity, empathy).

TYPE OF QUESTIONS

There are two types of questions: "Create a XX" or "Improve YY", but they are both used to test the same skills.

The content of the questions varies by the type of company. Interviewers from mid-large companies are more likely to ask questions about general products. Interviewers from startups are more likely to ask questions related to their own product/industry.

WHAT WOWS INTERVIEWERS

Extras

Interviews consider "extras" like solution design, risks, and launch to be impressive. In this area, startup interviewers focus on executing on the idea for this portion of the interview (e.g., how would you build it?). Large companies also focus on executing and building the idea, but also delve into variations of the solution, risks, stakeholder management, etc.

Below is the rough amount of time each interviewer spent on each part of the interview when they provided their ideal answers:

- 30%: user brainstorming and problem prioritization
- 30%: solution brainstorming and prioritization
- 40%: solution design, risks, and extras

This is a very high-level generalization and varies by company size and interviewer. For example, interviewers from small companies prioritized solution design and execution while large companies prioritized user brainstorming and problem identification. Read the chapters on what startup interviewers value and what large company interviewers value to learn more.

A director of product at Google had the following to say:

Problem, solution brainstorming, then picking solution is great and it's really important to get the problem and user right. You must nail that. If you have time, it's impressive if you can go through everything else like designs, thoughtful risks, launch strategy, success metric tracking, technical challenges, competitor reactions, and me probing you for other considerations.

Compelling solution

A compelling solution is a product that solves the problem you laid out earlier.
It comes from choosing a burning problem and finding the logical solution to
it. It is hard to create a compelling solution to a boring/unimpactful problem.
One Facebook product manager said:

> *At the end of the interview, if I can say 'I wish that would exist in the
> world' or 'I would definitely use that', it does not matter if they made
> mistakes to get there, I would give them a pass.*

WHAT PUTS OFF INTERVIEWERS

Standard frameworks

Following a standard framework can be irritating for interviews because it is
very boring, and it does not show critical thinking skills. One Stripe product
manager was particularly vocal about this:

> *The interview is to test if you know when to use certain tactics to
> break down problems, which is a fundamental product manager
> skillset. If you are saying I am going to use some dumb framework,
> I'm already getting disengaged.*

Not moving fast enough

It is incredibly rude for interviewers to interrupt you, so it is going to be hard
for them to speed you up if you are rambling or if you are not deciding fast
enough. 70% of ideal answers for product design were done in 20 minutes.

Remember, none of the interviewers optimized for speed. In fact, they prioritized it the least in their evaluation of candidates. By targeting clarity/concise-
ness, your time automatically decreases.

APPROACH

1. During the interview, show all Design Fundamentals (see section on De-
    sign Fundamentals).

2. While prepping, spend time thinking about various types of users and their problems.
3. While prepping, practice brainstorming ideas/products that you wish existed in the world.
4. Always think of wide then deep. Wide when thinking about users, then pick one. Wide when thinking about problems, then pick one. Wide when thinking about solutions, then pick one.

Design Fundamentals

Below is the framework that ~100% of interviewers followed to answer product design questions. Use this framework mindfully. The product managers who provided the ideal answers followed this pattern because it allowed them to create a great product: a creative solution for the biggest pain point of an important user.

Below is the order they followed. Each step corresponds to a chapter in the Design Fundamentals section.

1. **Goal and context setting:** Understand goal.
2. **User brainstorming and prioritization:** List at least three users and understand their top priorities/complaints and pick one user.
3. **Problem-brainstorming and prioritization:** List at least two major pains for the chosen user and pick one problem (helpful to draw a user journey, 70% of ideal answers had one).
4. **Solution brainstorming:** List three solutions.
5. **Solution prioritization:** Prioritize and pick 1 solution.
6. **Solution design:** Pitch the product vision and design solution.
7. **Do extras** (e.g., state risks, thoughtful risks, launch strategy, success metric tracking, technical challenges, build steps, testing, and competitor reactions).

User then Problem or Problem then User?

It can be confusing to determine if you need to first brainstorm and pick a problem or brainstorm and pick a user. Generally, problem and user identification are very intertwined.

As a rule, almost always start by brainstorming and picking a user first.

For example, "Design a camera for seniors" already has the user identified, so we can dive right into the problems for seniors, right? Unfortunately, no.

There are seniors in old homes, seniors in residences, seniors in hospitals. We have seniors who are 65–75, 75–85, and 85–90+. There are also seniors in developed countries with good infrastructure and seniors in developing countries with terrible support structures. Their needs are extremely different. Having thought of all these possibilities, you can pick a user/senior that you think would have the most problems. For example, you can pick seniors in old homes in developing countries as they are a large group, struggle to fulfill basic needs more than seniors in developing countries, and you may be a bit more familiar with them.

You can also get a problem-centric prompt like "design a better coffee maker." In this case, if you immediately start identifying problems with the coffee maker, you will most likely identify them for yourself (e.g., "waking up, I wish it was just ready"). It is much more helpful to start with the user. You can start with coffee makers for businesses, people in homes, people in malls/on the go. The needs vary significantly depending on the user you pick. A business prioritizes speed and volume, a person drinking coffee at home prioritizes cost and taste, people in malls probably prioritize convenience and experience. Each user would thus have vastly different pain points.

Strategy Answer Patterns

TYPE OF QUESTIONS

Product managers from startups, medium, and large companies ask this question. These are the types of questions and their associated frequency:

- Launch/new entry (60%) (e.g., Would you create your own TV if you were Google?)
- Buy competitor/partner (30%) (e.g., Would you partner with Ford if you were Cruise?)
- Other (10%) (e.g., What do you think are the biggest tech trends next year?)

WHAT WOWS INTERVIEWERS

Considering users in high-level strategy

Making high-level strategic decisions based on user preferences is what senior/ lead/group product managers do regularly. If you can understand minute user preferences and be able to scale them to an industry level, that is very impressive. A Dropbox product manager provided an example to illustrate the point:

> *Should Dropbox build their own task management/note taking app? The dumb, but common, answer would be focusing on industry trends around online collaboration/note taking. The logical analysis of that market would be that there is enough saturation. If anything, Dropbox should just buy a company or should focus on other things, like copying Google Docs or Sheets. However, if you look at our users and our goal of online collaboration, most of our users live in their note tools. And users care about seamless interoperability. If we just bought a company and tried to integrate it, we would not get a seamless experience. If we built one out, maybe we would not increase storage, and maybe not as high usage initially, but we would allow people to work better together and make our platform stickier. Then you build an argument from there.*

WHAT PUTS OFF INTERVIEWERS

Using a strategy/business framework

Following a standard framework can be irritating for interviews because it is very boring, and it does not show critical thinking skills. For strategy questions, it can be particularly tempting to deal with the inherent ambiguity by defaulting into a common framework (e.g., Porter's 5 Forces). You can get to a much better answer by focusing on and solving the main user's pain points.

Another downside of using strategy/business frameworks is that almost none have a section on user preferences. Without hitting this key part, you risk staying too high level.

APPROACH

Actual interview question when Snap was much more popular: Should Snap launch payments? Answers are taken from an ideal answer and synthesized.

1. Set goal and high-level context for company (most important step).

    Snap's overall goal is to connect people and allow them to show their true selves. Given its decreasing usage, it should focus on increasing its current engagement with users and making sure more of their lives happen in the Snap ecosystem. Snap needs to get more sticky.

2. Discuss high-level industry trends (larger industry trends, strategic trends or costs).

    Payments are becoming easier across the spectrum and several other players are entering or dominating, like Venmo and Facebook. People already use Venmo and Snap separately, but payments could be an opportunity to make Snap stickier.

3. Pick one high-level subset of users that would be relevant (e.g., new users, current users, high-value customers, acquired company's customers).

    When I am thinking about increasing stickiness and usage, I do not think new users are as relevant. I want to make current users stickier, so I am going to focus on their problems around payments.

4. Provide high-level overview of users (e.g., What do they like/dislike? Who are they?).

    Our current users use Snap about once daily, and value three key pieces: privacy, transience, and fun. Whatever we choose to do needs to continue to follow these principles. We could think about branching out into new experiences that are not immediately transient (i.e., go away) but that is a topic for another time. Now that we are branching into a tangential service like payments, we need to continue to follow those principles.

5. Identify biggest pain points related to the problem at hand and identify current methods users must solve the problem (e.g., using competitor product, using a hack).

Payments has been pretty easily solved by Venmo. But the problem with Venmo is that your payments are public and shared with everybody. And even on other platforms, there is no way to not record a payment permanently. For example, if I pay someone on PayPal, then that would be recorded in my PayPal and theirs. If I wanted to send a payment that was obfuscated, I would have to resort to crypto (and even that would have a record). The only real option is cash. I think there's an opportunity to build a cash-like, no-record, digital payments provider.

6. Identify opportunity for company to solve (e.g., fits in company goals, benefit to getting it right).

    If Snap does this, it could become incredibly sticky in another category while keeping its experience private, transient, and fun. In addition to peer-to-peer payments, it could open a whole new category of experiences where people could pay for events/channels for private content or services. We have 300M daily users currently on Snap and reasonably 1 in 30 would want to use discrete payments immediately, so we would start off with 10M users. While this is low for a payments platform, based off our pain points discussion, we could expect that number, especially we create new categories around paid events and images.

7. Decide.

    I think Snap should build a discrete payments platform as it would create a new category in the market and solve a need that digital platforms do not satisfy at all currently.

8. Do extras (e.g., next steps, competitor reaction, launch strategy.

    While this is a really clever and compelling solution, there would be 2 major risks with this solution. Number 1, I'm not sure if it will be legally allowed. This could facilitate a lot of criminal activity, like money laundering. We can mitigate this by checking with lawyers on the feasibility and then putting in transfer limits. Number 2, I think it might take a while for us to build a payments and financial transfer platform. To mitigate this risk, we should find payment partners who would be willing to share their platform or APIs.

TYPE OF QUESTIONS

Most startups do not seem to ask this question at all. Large companies ask it sometimes. Most often, interviewers don't ask analytical questions explicitly but instead want you to include analytical thinking into your product design or strategy answers.

If you are pressed for time, do not worry about prepping for this type of question. In particular, do not worry about prepping for market calculation/approximation, it seems to happen rarely and if it does, it is usually not arbitrary estimation questions (e.g., how many ping pong balls in a school bus) because those are extremely useless.

This is the distribution for the type of questions:

- Pick a goal/metric (50%) (e.g., "If you were the product manager on Tik-Tok, what would be your success metrics?")
- Diagnostic (40%) (e.g., "Since yesterday, Facebook Pages usage is down 10%, what happened?")
- Market calculation/approximation (10%) (e.g., "Calculate how many autonomous cars could be sold in the US").

WHAT WOWS INTERVIEWERS

Stakeholders

Often, candidates just focus on the end-user and forget that most products are marketplace-based. While ~20% of candidates identified stakeholders, only ~5% of candidates incorporated the implications of stakeholders in their answer (both for analytical and product design questions), which is shockingly low. It is important to pick a metric/goal that accounts for all stakeholders.

Counter metrics

When you select a metric, it is important to accurately account for downsides. A counter metric is something companies measure to make sure they do not overoptimize solely on their main metric. Apparently, about 80% of candidates either don't pick a counter metric or pick an inaccurate one.

For each success metric, come up with a good counter metric that would convince you that you are not simply plugging one hole with another.—Facebook Product Design VP

WHAT PUTS OFF INTERVIEWERS

Unmeasurable metrics

Picking metrics that cannot be measured (e.g., picking "leases signed" for Craigslist apartment listings when Craigslist does not track that) is useless, but quite common. Almost 80% of candidates select one unmeasurable metric at some point in their interview.

Lack of structure

The lack of a common structure for analytical questions means that candidates often resort to following a haphazard approach to analytical questions or to diagnostic questions. For diagnostic questions, that could be asking random questions and for metric setting, it could be just naming random high-level goals. That is a red flag for the interview. If you encounter an issue on the job, instead of prioritizing potential causes and being strategic about your analysis, you might just continually ask your engineers and data scientists random questions.

Read through the Approach parts of this chapter to learn more.

Forgetting the goal

For the metric setting questions, interviewers do not particularly care for the "right" metric as much as they care about the reasoning for picking a particular metric. The justification needs to be logical and delineate the logic from a high-level goal to a specific metric. A Coinbase product manager provides a great example of working backward from the overall goal:

Say you are the product manager of Tinder and I ask you for your top goal. The overall goal of Tinder is to start relationships. So, the ideal goal to measure against would probably be something around the number of dates completed through the platform. To work backwards, the only thing you can measure is conversations started. It is hard to measure if a conversation actually led to a date (you can potentially measure % of conversations that end in phone numbers). So, your top metric is # of conversations started. Most people say something too high level like # of matches, # users, % of profile completed, daily users, etc. because they are not working backwards from the goal.—Coinbase product manager

Misusing A/B tests

It is extremely common for candidates new to product management to say they will use "A/B tests" for their product. Before you propose that, be clear a) if you can do an A/B test and b) if the results would be relevant. A Facebook director provided an example:

So often, candidates will say 'I'll do an A/B test' because they think that is what we want to hear. If you say that, clearly state your control and variable states, metric to-be-measured, associated timeline, and hypothesis. Most often, doing an A/B test does not actually work or answer the question. For example, an A/B test on a Facebook Portal design is kind of dumb. It is so wasteful to set up two different manufacturing lines just to A/B test. Or another example, an A/B test on voice features in Messenger. What if one person does not have access to a cool beta feature that their friend can access during a call? That is going to suck for the other person, why would we do something like that?

Every time I hear something like that, I just know I cannot pass this person, because they are just saying product manager things.

APPROACH FOR DIAGNOSTIC

The approach to solving a diagnostic correctly seems to be just asking a) relevant questions in a b) structured manner. Do not just ask question after question, state a hypothesis, and revise it with each question. Below are the paths that most product managers followed to find the issue:

- Look for recent changes shipped by other teams.
- Check the tool to make sure it is accurate.

- Check the underlying data to make sure it is accurate.
- Look back into history for any patterns in the data.
- Consider recent changes you shipped.
- Consider any changes that your company may have introduced outside of the product.
- Look for changes in user behavior or customer trends.
- Conduct competitive analysis.
- Look for macroeconomic or geographical changes.

APPROACH FOR ESTIMATION

This question seems to be exceedingly rare, and rarely does the interviewer actually expect the candidate to calculate the numbers in their head.

1. If the question requires some amount of strategy, state a reasonable direction (e.g., autonomous car sales in US).
2. Lay out equation to answer question.
3. Make assumptions for some of the numbers.
4. Start calculating (ask if you can use a calculator).
5. Validate if the number makes sense.
6. Revise number or other assumptions if necessary.
7. State implications.

APPROACH FOR PICK A GOAL/METRIC

Example: "Pick metrics for Facebook Pages," answered by Facebook product manager

1. Think of a company's overall goal/high-level context.

   Facebook's overall goal is to create communities.

2. List stakeholders/users and understand their top priorities and pain points.

   There are three main actors: Page Creators (Businesses, Artists, etc.), Page Followers, and Brand Marketers (paid page maintainers for artists, businesses). As we are focused on creating communities and authentic connections, I want to focus on the creators and followers. I think they are both equally important. However, there are already a lot of pages on Facebook, but extraordinarily little engagement and very few followers. So, the bigger problem is engaging followers.

3. List at least two major actions for user.

    The main things that a page creator does is a) create a page and b) add content/refresh content on the page. The main things that a follower does is a) follow the page and b) engage with content on the page.

4. Prioritize which are the most important actions to achieve the high-level goal.

    As we said, the main problems aren't around lack of page creation necessarily, its more with the lack of engagement around the page. This might be because not enough pages create good content and the followers not engaging with the content, creating a negative feedback loop with less incentive for creators to push new content. So, the most important actions are a) followers engaging with content on page and b) creators adding content to a page.

5. Create metrics for those actions.

    The metrics that define those actions are for a) number of likes per post on a Facebook page and b) number of posts created per page per month. By increasing these two, I would increase overall engagement and hit our overall goal of creating better communities.

6. Add counter and high-level metrics.

    Of course, I would still focus on high-level metrics like i) number of pages created, ii) number of overall page follows, and iii) number of inactive pages. But I would prioritize the two ones I laid out earlier.

Metrics measured by each company

Interviewers were asked for the metrics and goals that their companies measured. The product managers that were interviewed did not want to provide an answer in case it would be perceived as the "correct" answers nor were they willing to reveal their company's top metrics/goals as that would be a direct breach of trust of their company. However, they were willing to provide the best answers they had heard for metrics or ones that were closest to what they measured. The smaller companies were willing to divulge their metrics.

Zoom metrics in order

1. Total meeting minutes
2. Paid users and revenue
3. Unique monthly active participants (not users)
4. Zoom Platform usage (e.g., payments, events, apps)

Facebook Newsfeed metrics in order

1. Total minutes spent on app/website per month
2. Number of content engagements (e.g., reactions, article clicks) per user
3. # of unique daily users

Google mobile app metrics in order

1. Total number of searches
2. Daily users
3. Time spent on app
4. Photo searches (new feature)

Insurance Series D-startup in order

1. Claims Ratio KPI measures the number of claims in a period and divides that by the earned premium for the same period.
2. The Average Cost per Claim KPI measures how much your organization pays out for each claim filed by your customers.
3. The Net Income Ratio measures how effective your organization is at generating profit on each dollar of earned premium. This KPI is used to measure the profitability of your organization and is primarily used for internal comparison.
4. The Percentage of Sales Growth KPI measures the amount of policy renewals and new policy sales over a set period. The renewal ratio measures the number of insured clients that stay enrolled in a program after the initial coverage period expires. New policies include any clients purchasing coverage for the first time or returning after an extended period.
5. Loss ratio.

YouTube metrics in order

Desired user actions:

1. Likes on videos
2. Watching videos
3. Commenting on videos

Associated metrics:

- Average number of likes clicked per user
- Average video watch time per user
- Average number of comments per user

Counter metrics:

One pitfall: comments are not necessarily a positive user metric. While commenting users are engaged users, they may be frustrated, offended, or disgusted with the content they are viewing. To mitigate this concern, it'd be helpful to use sentiment analysis tools for comments to check if these comments are generally positive or negative in nature.

Another pitfall: watch time isn't necessarily a positive user metric, when taken to the extreme. Of course, it is beneficial to YouTube to have engaged users on the platform, but many users are nearly addicted to their YouTube viewing habits. If users feel like their time spent on YouTube is a waste, or that they can't help but watch YouTube instead of accomplishing their important life tasks, then perhaps YouTube's attractive influence is actually a downside.

Favorite Product Answer Patterns

WHAT WOWS INTERVIEWERS

Strong product sense

By asking this question, interviewers are looking to understand what you think makes a good product. Interviewers are more interested in your justification than in your product selection. It is important to pick a good product as it will allow you to provide an extremely detailed and compelling justification. Your justification will reveal your design priorities and taste.

You are almost definitely going to get asked this at some point in all your interviews. About 80% of product managers agree that they ask this 'extremely often' to judge product sense. There are several types of this question, which is covered later, but you should aim to have at least one favorite product.

A Stripe product manager expanded on the importance of this question:

> *When I ask what is your favorite product, I am still looking for the same traits around user empathy and clarity like in the other questions. But on top of that, I am really looking for real product sense. This is a really useful question because I can judge what you think makes a really good product.*

Improvements

The next step to providing a favorite product is providing solid recommendations for improvement. It is hard to improve a product that is already considered great, especially with no context around data, usage, etc. So, if you can suggest improvements that are compelling, that is very impressive. A VP Product of a Series D-startup explained:

> *Picking a great product is the start. I can really judge deep product sense when a candidate can give me strong recommendations. Especially if I use the product and I would use the proposed features, it is such an immediate pass.*

WHAT PUTS OFF INTERVIEWERS

Several patterns seem to put off interviewers. In fact, this is probably the question that received the most feedback from interviewers on "what makes you not like a candidate?"

Trying to be niche

Interviewers value creativity as the least important trait for almost all questions and that continues to apply here. Interviewers do not really value creativity that highly for this question. As in, there is no value in trying to pick a creative/niche product. If you are pitching a unique/niche product, pitch it because you think it is genuinely the best product, not because you think there is value in picking something niche. A Google product manager was particularly adamant about this point:

> *I really do not need someone to pick an obscure product or teach me a new product. There are only a few good products out there. I detest when interviewers say 'I like it when a candidate teaches me something' because it sends the wrong signal to candidates. Often, these interviewers are just young. Once you do 500+ interviews in your career, you start to see common 'favorite products'.*

Not providing justification

Be thoughtful about your justification as that matters significantly more than the product you choose. Pick any product that you like. As was covered earlier, picking a good product is just the start of the question. It is more important to spend time on providing a clear justification. A Dropbox Director product manager provided an example:

> *Sometimes, it can be helpful for you to identify a niche product. But only because that is one of the few products that is designed just the way you like, and you can provide a great justification. Do not say some random to-do list software because you think I do not know much about it. After you leave and I search it up, and I think it is a bad product, I'll think you have terrible judgement. People think they should not say Google because it is popular and not niche. But that is completely the wrong judgement, Google is a bad product to pick because there is only so much you can say about why you like it: 'minimal, fast, easy to use'. Pick something you can really dive into, like Dropbox, or even the Google mobile app.*

Trying to please

Some candidates choose to pick the product of the company they're interviewing for. If you really love their product, then choose it. But be incredibly careful as product managers can perceive you as giving an "easy" answer. A Series C startup Group Product Manager had a strong reaction:

I do not need you to tell my product is great`. Because if you do, you know I am going to rip into you to make sure that you are telling the truth. And if you pass, that is great.

APPROACH

1. Before the interview, think about at least three products: favorite software product, favorite hardware/physical product, and least favorite product.
2. Explain the goal of product and a high-level description of how it hits the goal.
3. Explain its users and their pain points. Ensure that you do this step so that you start by explaining the problem and then move on to explain its novel solution. Apparently ~50% candidates skip the user and pain point description and start with an in-depth description of the solution.
4. Provide more detail as to how its distinctive/novel features solve those problems (over competitors or other solutions).
5. Pitch its improvements. For this question, imagine you are the product manager of the product. How could the user experience or user interface be improved? How could this product engage more, or expand to a new customer segment? How would you adjust the product's 10-year vision?

Product manager interviewers' favorite product

Because of the excitement around this question, a subset of the product manager interviewers were asked a follow-up question for their favorite product. Here are the results:

- Microsoft Teams x5
- Google Keep x3
- Roblox x3
- Messenger x2
- Notion x2
- AirTable x2
- Hubspot x2

There are two takeaways for this. The main takeaway was that there was almost no commonality. The second, but very minor, was that note-taking and task management tools seemed to be common.

So, do not try to guess your interviewer's favorite software product or a popular and cool product. Clearly, they all disagree.

Pick a product that you genuinely like, even if it is not popular. Again, it does not really matter what you pick, it matters a lot more to have a strong justification. For example, lots of people would disagree that Teams is a great product. But for some, it meets their needs exactly (it has more than $10\times$ users than Slack). The whole point of product management is to build products for a specific subset of users. They are judging your product sense, not trying to validate if you know the coolest product of the month.

Other Question Patterns

There are very few other types of questions apart from the ones we've discussed. It is exceedingly rare to get these questions, so it is not recommended to spend too much time preparing for them.

There are no "What wows interviews" or "What puts off interviewers" sections for these questions as there was not enough data to analyze patterns for these types of questions.

There are three types of "other" questions:

- Launch (e.g., launch Amazon Go in Mexico)
- Build (e.g., now that you have designed the app, how would you work with your engineers to build it?)
- Price (e.g., price Google Chromebook)

APPROACH FOR LAUNCH

In general, for launch questions, it is important to always summarize and signpost even more.

1. Scope down the area immediately. Launch questions are often broad (e.g., launch Amazon Go in Mexico), so be clear as to a) which product you are launching, b) in what time frame, c) for what area, and d) with what budget.

*This is a broad question. I am going to focus on these three aspects, is
that all right? Or do you want me to focus on other things?*

2. Set a business goal.

   *"Hit user goal in this amount," "Reach this much general awareness,"
   "Get these many repeat users."*

3. Understand users (e.g., Why are they using the product? Who? Where?,
   How to reach?). Most important question is "how reach?"

   *For Amazon Go in Mexico, I think it is important to start with ur-
   banities and young and upcoming professionals. So, I'll start with
   dense cities. We can then sequentially expand to the other users, and
   then plan different launches. If we want to reach the other folks faster,
   maybe we can use partnerships to launch quicker.*

4. Phase users and associated launch. Mention you'd work with your marketing team on phasing.
5. Plan pre-launch (e.g., metrics, user segmentation and associated marketing, pricing, partnerships).
6. Gather data or talk to users (e.g., run focus groups, user observations) to
   verify launch plan.
7. During launch (e.g., track metrics, run marketing, support for launch).
8. Post launch (e.g., analyze metrics, action metrics, ensure stakeholder hap-
   piness).

APPROACH FOR BUILD

This build process will vary by company, but ensure that you talk about col-
laborating with (not dictating to) your engineers throughout all these steps.

1. Break product down into user stories.
2. Do wireframes for each user flow.
3. Convert stories into requirements with dev estimates in grooming ses-
   sions with engineering.
4. Plan out story points and slot requirements into sprint schedules.
5. Attend daily standups to unblock problems.
6. At the end of each sprint, prioritize for the next sprint and do a sprint on
   how to be more efficient.

APPROACH FOR PRICING

Pricing questions are very interactive because there are so many assumptions that need to be made. The approach below is more of a range of options you or the interviewer could choose to pursue.

1. Set business goal (either market share or profit)
2. State of market (e.g., growing/mature, competitor pricing)
3. Types of pricing setup (e.g., value based, cost plus, competition)
4. Types of offerings (e.g., tiered, a la carte, subscription, free trial, razor blade model)
5. Differentiation (their advantage, our advantage)
6. Recommendation

Design Fundamentals

Design Fundamentals Introduction

<u>Aim:</u> Mastering these fundamentals will help you in behavioral, product design, product strategy, and analytical questions.

<u>Description:</u> Design Fundamentals dives into the fundamental skills (e.g., user selection, goal selection, problem selection) that interviewers test for. There are seven chapters, each associated with a skill that interviewers considered fundamental:

- Delivery/communication
- Goal and context setting
- User brainstorming and prioritization
- Problem-brainstorming and prioritization
- Solution brainstorming
- Solution prioritization
- Solution design.

These skills may look really familiar because they match the exact steps to answer a product design question. Product design questions are very common because they allow the interviewer to test all these skills.

We will apply these principles to an example done by an Amazon principal product manager for "How would you improve Alexa to increase usage?" If you want, try the example yourself now or after you the "Approach" part of each chapter and compare your answer.

Each chapter has the following structure:

- What wows interviewers
- What puts off interviewers
- Approach
- Applying to improve Alexa problem
- Other: Interesting Ideas/etc.

Delivery Patterns

Delivery is the most important skill that the interviewer will be testing you on. Previous chapters have expounded on its importance in great detail, so we will not go through the justification here again. Focus your practice on getting enough of the content correct and then immediately transition to refining your delivery.

WHAT WOWS INTERVIEWERS

Detailed documentation

In video interviews, use a shared doc to document your thoughts clearly. As one Stripe product manager explained:

> *It is really easy to follow someone's thought process if I can just see what they are typing. I can also scroll back to make sure that I understood previous points. I think I am going to do shared docs even when I do in-person interviews.*

Only ~5% of candidates were able to replicate the level of clarity and detail that is present in a high-level product requirement document during the interview. One Dropbox product manager director added to the survey results:

> *The solution at the end should looks like a basic product requirement document you'd write for your product.*

Assertiveness/confidence

Confidence inspires interviewers to trust and believe in you. Interviewers will not ding you for being nervous. That is very normal in an interview. However, if you can act like the stress does not bother you and you're playing in your element, the interviewer will be impressed.

Interviewers might even make the situation a bit tense or stressful. They're not trying to make you fail. They are testing to see your reaction under pressure from a difficult customer or colleague. If they wanted you to fail, they would never have agreed to interview you. Nobody is twisting their arm to force them to interview you. They are interviewing you because they want to.

Interviewers have mentioned that they trust the answer more when a candidate is confident. One Uber Group Product Manager said:

> *I remember passing this one dude who was not amazing at interviewing, but during the interview, he was so confident that I was convinced his solution was amazing. Only after I looked at my notes a while later did I realize it was good but not amazing, but he was so jazzed about the idea and the problem that it convinced me.*

Engaging and summarizing

Signposting is the act of summarizing progress made so far as well as providing an indication of where you are headed. It should feel like seeing a signpost while driving on a highway—X km remaining of your destination. About 90% of ideal answers had signposts every ~3 minutes.

Almost all ideal answers also had a "check-in" right after the signpost. A check-in is used to engage the interviewer with phrases like "does that make sense to you?," "let me know if you want to head in another direction." A Microsoft Group Manager summarized the importance of signposting and checking in:

> *If you think you are signposting too much, you are signposting the right amount.*

Conciseness

About 90% of ideal answers had less than two sentences per justification. When you're explaining your points, remember to take only 1–2 sentences to explain your reasoning per point. Offer to expand after you've provided your short explanation, but don't jump into a long explanation right at the beginning. A Microsoft Principal product manager said:

> *I literally get bored when people give me a whole essay about one small decision. I cannot even interrupt you to say that I understand because that'd be rude. Either you are bad at communicating or you are explaining a breakthrough concept. And it is very likely that you are the first.*

WHAT PUTS OFF INTERVIEWERS

Speaking too fast

It is normal to be more hurried and speak faster when you're nervous. However, the interviewer will have trouble following your thoughts if they're too fast. Always remember that interviewers ranked speed as the least important trait they're looking for.

Practice speaking at your normal pace in mock interviews. In your interview, just imagine you're working with a new colleague and continue to speak normally. If you want to get extremely precise in your practice, research has shown that speaking more than ~110 words per minute can be considered fast.

APPROACH

1. Record and hear yourself for 2–3 mocks. About 60% of experienced product managers mentioned they had recorded and reviewed their own work when prepping for interviews.
2. Phrase your work around "us" rather than "me." About 70% of ideal answers had their questions around collaboration (e.g., "do you like our direction" NOT "do you like my direction").
3. Enumerate your points. 100% of ideal answers had numbered points. Aim to write down at least two points before speaking.
4. If you make a mistake, do not panic, but instead be clear about your mistake and revise your solution/pain point. Read Recovering from mistakes.
5. Signpost every ~3 minutes. DON'T state the exact actions you have done, instead state the results of the action.

NOT: "I've done the user segmentation, and now I am going to solution design."

"So, we've understood that [insert user] cares the most about [problem], so now let's figure out how to solve [problem] while making sure the [stakeholders] also like the solution."

"Okay, so we've understood that moms' most burning pain point when trying to find a crib and other baby products is trusting reviews, let's figure out what solutions we can come up with. "

6.   Check in right after you signpost.

   "Just wanted to check in, does that make sense to you?"

   "Would love your thoughts on our direction so far."

   "Happy to dive into whichever topic you prefer, but I am going to pick this one for two reasons. "

   "I think we've spent a lot of time on [the previous section], so I would like to wrap [this section] up fairly quickly so that we can spend more time on [next section], does that make sense?"

Recovering from mistakes

You will make mistakes during your interview process. It is important to practice pivoting and correcting after a mistake so that you are not flustered during the interview. Almost 30% of the ideal answers had a "mistake" or a turn/pivot that the interview took.

It helps to have gone through the interview quickly so that, even when you make a mistake, you can either reverse or change course and still have time to complete the interview. As mentioned in this chapter and What interviewers value, interviews do not particularly value speed. However, by being concise and clear throughout the interview, you can hit all the required parts of the answer fairly quickly and leave time for mistakes/pivots.

First, when you realize you have made a mistake, do not apologize. Almost none of the interviewers apologized or admitted a mistake. Instead, they framed the mistake as a learning opportunity. A Sr. product manager from Square made a mistake in their ideal answers and said:

> *Looks like we may have taken a turn that wasn't super productive, I would love to take a step back and review our progress so far and take a turn towards something better.*

Second, continue to be confident. Mistakes are common in interviews. Surprisingly, the large majority (90%) of interviewers appreciated when a candidate called out a gap in their own logic. It shows that the candidate is thinking critically and continuously double-checking their logic. A product manager lead from Facebook said:

> *I actually love when a candidate says 'I may have made a misstep here, let me revise this'. Because sometimes, I may have already caught it but just waited for them to catch it. As long as they're not making a mistake every second, I really don't ding a candidate for making a mistake.*

> *At end of the interview: "I am glad we changed direction in the middle of the interview, this solution is amazing, I would actually definitely use it."*

If the interviewer points out a mistake/fault in logic, accept the guidance graciously, but still don't admit a mistake. Pretend the interviewer is a colleague trying to help. Accept their suggestion and modify your approach. When we pointed out a mistake in the ideal answer of a Sr. product manager interviewer from Google, they said:

> *That's actually a great suggestion and you are right, I should modify my approach, great insight.*

WHAT WOWS INTERVIEWERS

Tying back

It seems it is a bit difficult to "wow" interviewers in the goal and context setting. In the later parts of the solution, it can be impressive/rare to consistently tie back to the goal. A Square product manager said:

> *So, now that we have picked our user and we are now picking a specific problem, just want to signpost really quickly. Our initial goal was to increase daily users, so when I go through to pick a problem, I am going to pick the problem that will draw the most daily users (not necessarily revenue, ads, downloads, reviews, referrals, etc.).*

Remember stakeholders

Taking stakeholders into account in later parts of the interview. Apparently, only ~5% of candidates incorporate stakeholder concerns in their answer (both for analytical and product design), which is shockingly low. This is especially important in marketplace questions.

WHAT PUTS OFF INTERVIEWERS

Jumping to assumptions

You need to make assumptions to set context for the problem. However, don't make too many unnecessary assumptions upfront. Ideal answers only had ~2 assumptions upfront and they were usually about a) budget and b) timeline.

APPROACH

1. Instead of jumping right into questions, take some time to set your own context and make assumptions and confirm them.

   Not: "So what is our goal here?"

Ask: "Since we are a Series C startup and we just raised a significant round, I think our goal is still around usage growth, and while we want to keep an eye on expenses, we are not too concerned at this time, is that correct?"

2. Make assumptions that will help you later in designing your solution, not constrain it.
3. Ensure you understand the exact scope of the question, and potentially even broaden it.

   Not: "I am going to assume that it is an app."

   Ask: "Great, so we are making a solution for decreasing screen time on phones, I am not going to say it is an app right now as we might even explore other alternatives like a physical safe, so let me dive into the type of users."

4. Ensure you understand the exact scope of the question, and potentially even broaden it.

   Not: "I am going to jump into users that could use this backpack."

   Ask: "You said that you want to 'improve backpacks', do you mean just the two-strap bag that you put on your back? Or would it be anything that allows us to hold things in a bag, like a suitcase or handbag? Want to make sure that we are potentially considering all solutions."

5. Identify stakeholders by taking a marketplace view of everything (see Stakeholder Identification below)
6. Tie in goals/stakeholders for the rest of the interview

Consumer vs Enterprise Goals

It is important to provide the right type of goal to the right type of company. Product managers from consumer companies and product managers from enterprises companies consistently provided different types of goals.

Consumer

Product managers from both large and small consumer companies stated similar goals:

- User engagement (e.g., Unique Visitors, New vs Returning Visitors, Pageviews, Time on Page, Pages per Session, Conversion Rate)
- User adoption (Active Users, Product Access, Average Time Spent with Product, Feature Adoption Rate)
- User retention (e.g., Customer Churn, Net Promoter Score, Customer Retention Rate, Average Order Value, Customer Lifetime Value)

Almost never did a consumer product manager mention monetization as a goal. It was perceived as a strong negative when a candidate mention it as a goal.

> *"Facebook's goal is about creating communities, so ensuring our groups and marketplaces and messages are more active is more important than for example, making sure people click on ads. I know someone cannot be a good fit if they come in just targeting ads, that is a bad user experience."—Facebook product manager*

Enterprise

Product managers from both large and small enterprise companies stated similar goals:

- Monetization
- Retention
- Customer Lifetime Value.

Stakeholder identification

Take a marketplace viewpoint on every problem and incorporate stakeholders later on in the interview.

A Flipkart product manager provided an example in using stakeholders when picking a solution:

> *As I pick this solution for healthcare payments for immigrant families, we want to make sure we are accounting for integration into*

> *insurance companies. As we discussed in the stakeholder section, in-surance companies benefit of obfuscation, a solution that requires their co-operation would be difficult to implement. So, I am going to focus on solutions that can be standalone.*

Again, apparently only ~5% of candidates effectively use stakeholders later in the interview. This is shockingly low considering almost every product has more than one important stakeholder. For example:

- Healthcare: doctors, insurance, patients
- Renting: visitors, hosts (Airbnb)
- Leasing: landlords, property managers, renters
- Ads: creators, advertiser, viewers

> *This might not be relevant for every problem, but it can help set use-ful context. If it is a hospital/healthcare product, identifying insur-ance companies as a key player is helpful for solution design and risk mitigation.—DoorDash product manager*

APPLYING TO EXAMPLE PROBLEM

"How would you improve Alexa to increase usage?," answered by Amazon prin-cipal product manager

I'm going to assume that our overall goal is to increase Alexa usage and the orders of products and services associated with Alexa (e.g., Echo).

There's a couple of stakeholders in the Alexa ecosystem:

- Alexa Skills creators
- Alexa users
- Alexa resellers (e.g., Walmart)

By improving our product, all of them will benefit with increased sales and usage.

WHAT WOWS INTERVIEWERS

Intuition to pick one compelling user

It is important to pick just one user, instead of resorting to building a product for a general user. About 80% of interviewers picked just one user in their ideal answers. A compelling user is a person/business/entity with a set of compelling problems. It can be hard to pick a compelling user with only a high-level understanding of their problems. The intuition to find the user with the most compelling problems is impressive because it is difficult to do. A Netflix product manager said:

> *Problems and users get really interesting when you pick a user and go deep. If you leave it at the high level, rarely do you get a compelling problem. Candidates think they can either pick a general user or do not have the intuition to pick a compelling user before diving into problems in detail.*

WHAT PUTS OFF INTERVIEWERS

Trying to brainstorm all users

Candidates often default to using a collectively exhaustive approach, which means (i.e., they try to analyze the entire universe of users). This often means candidates use a segmentation that does not apply to the problem. About 90% of ideal answers didn't have a collectively exhaustive list. An Uber product manager provided an example:

> *If I ask about a new ride-sharing product that syncs up with public transport such that you can seamlessly jump from Uber to bus and vice versa, do not tell me how old vs young people are going to use it. I want to throw myself out the window when someone starts a user segmentation with 'old, middle-age, and young'. Unless I am asking about an anti-aging product, do not talk to me about age. Or even 'very frequent, frequent, and non-frequent users'. I want to hear about office workers, students, disabled individuals, and shift workers. Their usage patterns and needs are extremely different.*

Forgetting businesses

Candidates often default to thinking about themselves, their friends, and their circles. This means that candidates focus on consumers and often forget businesses. Almost 50% of all ideal answers focused on business problems. B2B software businesses make up a significant part of software revenue per year (e.g., Microsoft, Stripe, Salesforce, Amazon Web Services, Google Cloud Platform). Just think: how many pieces of software do you use vs what a business would use? A Stripe product manager was quite exasperated:

> *People ALWAYS forget business! Add businesses to anything and you can most likely come up with a more creative and burning problem.*

APPROACH

1. Before your interview, spend time brainstorming example users (see Common users and high-level descriptions to get you started).
2. Pick users from various backgrounds. If you are just starting out, try to pick one user based on age (e.g., senior), one behavioral trait (e.g., runner), and one attitude (e.g., fashion). Do not do this in an interview setting, but it will help you figure out segmentation patterns that work for each question.
3. Provide 1–2 sentence high-level background on each user and their problems.
4. Ask the interviewer "is there anyone that you want me to pick?"
5. Pick a user based on your intuition for who would have the most burning problems.

> *For example, say you are thinking about solving the renting experience. Everybody has similar problems: price, location, look, landlord, and comfort/feel. But ask yourself, who would have the most severe ones? Probably international immigrants, as on top of the usual problems, they have additional ones as they do not know the language/country/culture and may be less affluent.*

> *Another example. For a better backpack, the problem has been solved to death for students, but has it been solved for office workers? If you even glance at a subway or bus, office workers spend a lot more on bags and probably suffer more back/shoulder pain in general. There is more room for improvement there.*

Common users and high-level descriptions

Develop a list with common demographics and their pain points. This will help you build empathy and pick compelling users during the interview.

> *It is so much easier to come up with compelling problems if you have spent time thinking of user problems before hand. Because then you can just take what you know about users/buyers (e.g., large businesses have trouble with employee onboarding, their employees often do not feel valued, etc.) and pair it with the current problem of say, selling recruiting software.—Shopify product manager*

Here's an extremely basic list to get you started:

- Young adults: are delivery services' largest customer, are ride-sharing's largest customer, are the demographic with the most mental health problems, often rent because they cannot own, more tech-savvy.
- Immigrants: typically less affluent but very hardworking, do not have professional network to find a job, do not understand local professional culture, often are students or have young kids.
- Runners/bikers: hard to run/bike in extreme weather (e.g., winter, hot weather), can be isolating, hard to eat enough to keep up calorie count.
- Small businesses: do not have enough standard processes (e.g., recruiting, HR), have minimal clarity on finances (e.g., financial projections), do not have enough financial capital in easy access.
- Children: need help on basic tasks, need constant supervision, can suffer mental health problems, are at risk of developing addictions to screens.
- Large businesses: hard to manage culture/HR at scale, must manage stakeholders, are not nimble enough, cannot adopt software quickly at scale, hard to speak with customers directly without large salesforce, hard to manage expenses.
- Vegans: hard to find vegan food at random restaurants, do not want to feel awkward in social settings, not enough vegan restaurants, hard to travel internationally
- Fashionable: hard to find/access hard to predict next-big-thing, can be frustrating to have to always have to buy new clothes to not re-wear old clothes
- Seniors: are generally lonely, cannot use tech, typically suffer health problems, have limited mobility (do not have driver's licenses), can be wealthy.

APPLYING TO EXAMPLE PROBLEM

"How would you improve Alexa to increase usage?", answered by Amazon principal product manager

Okay, we would like to start by talking about the types of users that are likely to buy voice-controlled assistant devices like the Amazon Echo, who they are, and what things they may want to do that the current Amazon Echo product does not support. After brainstorming on some use cases related to voice-controlled assistants, we would select the ones that I think would help achieve the goals if backed by a new feature.

The main current types of users of Alexa are:

- Families that are technology savvy and have mid- to high disposable incomes to buy non-essential electronic devices.
- Elderly parents of potential buyers (kids would be the buyers)
- Single individuals

Want to expand and think of new users:

- Retail stores
- Offices

Okay, we would like to take a minute to brainstorm possible use cases that have not been addressed by Amazon Echo for these three users yet.

Families:

- Do not have time to plan their meals, such as deciding what to cook, which ingredients to buy, and how to cook the meal.
- Assistance in choosing a recipe, buying ingredients, and step-by-step instructions on how to cook would save them time.
- Finding folks to service home
- Children learning a new language or skill.

Elderly:

- Remembering which medication to take, at what times, and in which order to take them.

- Forgetting key information, such as family information or situational awareness. For example, forgetting that you have two sons and they are visiting today.

Single individual:

- Public speaking coaching is something many professionals are interested.
- Having a personal trainer for exercising.
- Learning how to play an instrument. Could correct your wrong tones and allows you to be handsfree.

Retail stores:

- Service customers immediately
- Manage inventory seamlessly.
- Handle employee knowledge and concerns

Office workplace:

- Order food for the workplace
- Order requirements for the office (e.g., chair, monitor)

If our goal is to increase Amazon's overall revenue and increase Alexa's footprint, we want to target two things in our prioritization:

1. whitespace (most opportunity for Amazon to create new use cases) and
2. largest user category.

Based on these two factors, we think retail stores are the most interesting users/buyers in this scenario based on these two prioritization criteria.

We could have thousands of daily users using the retail store solutions even with only one buyer (one retail store). We also haven't really played in the business space before, so it has the most whitespace for new solutions.

A segment of the other users is already using Alexa. While we can think of some killer-use cases for them, we do not know if we'll drastically increase daily users, as we could with the business option.

WHAT WOWS INTERVIEWERS

- **Empathy.** 90% of large company product managers said that this section was the most important part of the interview.

  The best product are the ones that have the most compelling problems, this upfront is so important. The better you can articulate a problem that will compel users to go download this app, the better your solution will be.—LinkedIn Group Product Manager

- **Interesting synthesis.** About 80% of ideal answers had a "problem synthesis" that summarized the problem.

  It is like a nice little bow tie at the end of the section when a candidate can summarize the problem into a broader statement that we can use to brainstorm solutions. Instead of "to summarize, moms have a really tough time buying diapers," they say "so, we are going to reduce the time and effort it takes for busy, single moms to keep their babies' butts clean!"—LinkedIn product manager

WHAT PUTS OFF INTERVIEWERS

N/A. Interviewers did not have any frustrations with this section.

APPROACH

- Before your interview, explore a key user problem that you outlined in the previous chapter.

  This is probably the most important part of the interview. This is where I really know if the candidate can be a great product manager, can they nail the user's problems? Can they understand what makes the users tick? Can they pick the most burning pain point?—Stripe product manager

- If applicable, try to create a user journey for chosen user, 70% of ideal answers had a user journey.
- Discuss problems with current user choices (e.g., other backpacks are terrible for these reasons) or along the user journey.

> *People spend a lot of time thinking they have to come up with the fanciest problem or use case. While that would be impressive, it is more important that you follow a linear approach in picking your problems, so that you pick something that is mostly logical. At this stage, it is important to show empathy, not creativity.—Google product manager*

- Create prioritization framework. Often, this contains just one metric: the most burning problem for the user. But it can also include other factors. About 90% of startup product managers mentioned that they wanted the candidate to consider "alignment with company goals" when choosing a problem.
- Pick the problem.
- Summarize with a problem synthesis. A problem synthesis explains the core of the problem and creates an inspiring problem, usually by tying to a broader theme (e.g., why does this problem matter?)

> *"To summarize, people struggle with Spotify's personal profile and do not use it as much because it does not have that much functionality and does not allow you to share your interests" vs "So what we are focusing on is the way people represent their identify through music" when identifying problems with Spotify's personal profile setup.*

Example User Journey

Finding a doctor, by Tesla product manager

> *In this example, you can see that your user journey really does not need to be complicated or long, just logical. Depending on the user you pick, the most burning pain point would be different. For millennials, they know how to search and find, but transferring files is probably the biggest pain as that is done by paper.—Tesla product manager*

- Start/trigger: either I am already feeling sick or I am proactively looking for a new doctor (different levels of urgency)

- Searching/discovery
  - o Which match up with insurance companies?
  - o Who are close to me or my work?
- Investigating
  - o Reviews
  - o Co-pay/prices
- Calling/searching online for soonest appointments
- Confirming
- Transferring files between doctors

Going back to the earlier chapter about users, it is much easier to pick up compelling problems if you have a compelling user. For example, if we picked non-English speaking patients trying to find a doctor, then almost every stage is a goldmine of problems: searching, navigating the insurance loopholes, calling for appointments, checking language accessibility per clinic, etc.

Common phrases in problem-brainstorming

- "Key user need"
- "Do those make sense, or do you want me to elaborate on each of them as I would love to move on to [xxx]"
- "Before I think about features, I would love to understand what users care about in terms of [feature]"
- "What would they want in a [feature] and then we can think about how to satisfy that?"
- "I really feel like this is the burning pain point for this user."

APPLYING TO EXAMPLE PROBLEM

"How would you improve Alexa to increase usage?", answered by Amazon principal product manager

The problems would have to be centered around conversation, so between the customer and the employee or the employee and the customer.

- Fulfilling customer service requests
- Answering customer questions in-store
- Facilitating curbside pickup scenarios (e.g., instead of ordering ahead, can you order takeout through Amazon Echo in a drive-through?)

- Handling employee requests (e.g., paging for help over intercom vs asking Alexa to ping somebody)

Of all these use cases, I would prioritize the ones that are more likely to help achieve the goals stated earlier: to increase purchases of the Echo and increase purchases of products and services from other Amazon businesses. The use cases that would be aligned with these goals would be those that are important to the user and frequent enough for the user to want to buy the Amazon Echo. Ideally, they should also lead to the frequent purchase of products and services from Amazon.

Therefore my criteria for prioritizing the problems is:

1. targeting larger number of users
2. whether it can be reasonably done by Alexa

Based on these, I think answering customer service questions in-store would be the best problem to focus on. We can solve it with Alexa and it is an extremely important problem for retailers and for users, with many interactions per day.

So, we are going to help retailers better serve their customers by removing the friction of ad-hoc employee–customer questions, using Alexa.

Solution Brainstorming

WHAT WOWS INTERVIEWERS

Practical vs bold ideas

Interviewers from large companies and interviewers from small companies were impressed by different things. Big companies generally want big, bold ideas. Almost every product manager (90%) of large company products had crazy/moonshot ideas in their ideal answers. Large companies have resources, capital, and networks; they want to know that product managers can use all of them to push it forward. About 60% of product manager interviewers from large companies noted that they found it interesting when a candidate considered "gamification" in their solution brainstorming. A Google product manager said:

"Ultimately you really kill it when you have a great and creative solution at the end. Your structure matters a lot there and your overall approach should be linear, but to go from good to great, at the end you should have a solution that makes me go wow. That's when I know that I'll put it in as a strong hire."

On the other hand, small companies want practical, solid ideas. Almost no startup product manager (~0%) had answers with crazy/moonshot ideas. Some product managers mentioned that it can be refreshing to see crazy/moonshot ideas from candidates but not necessary. It is a waste of time to consider them as they do not have the resources to pursue them. About 80% of small company product managers said that this was the most important part of the interview. A Series B startup product manager said:

I want something genuinely practical here, not like a crazy idea, but something that works. I want to know that if I hire this girl, she's going to start producing on day 1, not have her head in the clouds.

APPROACH

1. To come up with cool ideas quickly, have a list of cool ideas that you build up before the interview. Find a list of interesting ideas below.
2. Pair the problem with the interesting ideas to come up with interesting solutions.
3. Aim to have three solutions and order them such that the first one is obvious, the second one is reasonable but creative, and the third one is a moonshot idea.

Interesting Ideas

Here are some ideas to kick off your list based on the ideal answers. You should create your own list.

- Suggested intelligent AI responses (e.g., your fridge suggests recipes)
- Intelligent cameras ((e.g., ability to extract specific information from captured images)
- AR/VR (e.g., making learning experiential and immersive)
- Always-aware assistant (e.g., AI hearing your conversation and then automatically populating search results on your phone)

- Gaming (e.g., chrome dinosaur game if you get an error)
- Personalization (e.g., a gift for a good friend)
- Messenger chat bot (e.g., AI girlfriend)
- Personal assistant (e.g., automates everything in your life, ordering food when you get home)
- Robotics (e.g., robot for personal care)
- Tinder type interface, swipe left swipe right (e.g., swiping left and right on the
- Marketplaces (e.g., Uber, Airbnb)

APPLYING TO EXAMPLE PROBLEM

> *"How would you improve Alexa to increase usage?", answered by Amazon principal product manager*

There are a couple of ways to solve this problem:

1. Alexa integrated into the company mobile app so that they can ask questions through there.
2. Buttons around the store that customers can press to ask Alexa questions.
3. Alexa service that you can just ask for all your orders and it instructs an employee to retrieve it.

Solution Prioritization

WHAT WOWS INTERVIEWERS

Answer first

About 70% of product managers appreciated when a candidate provided the answer first and then explained their reasoning. A Facebook product manager explained:

> *I hate when a candidate just starts talking about random trade-offs. Honestly, the best answers are when the candidate says up front, "this is my prioritization framework, give me a few minutes to think through my answer." Then thinks through and says, "this is the best solution" and then walks through their reasoning as to why. If you*

are just rambling, talking about each solution, it is hard to follow the train of thought.

Adopt a clear prioritization framework and apply it logically and sequentially to all ideas. Then, take time to think through your answer, pick the solution, and then walk the interviewer through it. A Facebook product manager

Using the appropriate framework

Product managers from both large and small companies wanted candidates to use a logical framework. Most candidates do this effectively.

To impress interviewers beyond the basic prioritization exercise, it can be helpful to mirror the interviewer's prioritization framework. In the ideal answers, product managers from large companies used different prioritization frameworks compared to product managers from small companies. About 90% of product managers from big companies seem to use "benefit to user" and "cost to user." There seem to be different variations of this, but the interviewers were less oriented around the time to develop, distribution, cost to develop, etc. About 80% of product managers from startups/medium companies seem to use "benefit to user" and "cost to develop."

The prioritization frameworks from these product managers seem to be more focused on "alignment with company goal" and the cost to distribute, time to develop, etc. In fact, interviewers from small companies noted that they were particularly impressed when candidates weighed these factors and chose solutions based on constrained resources. Read the chapter on What startup interviewers value for more information.

WHAT PUTS OFF INTERVIEWERS

Rambling

It can be disadvantageous to talk too much about each option. About 90% of ideal answers had less than two sentences per justification. A Series B startup product manager said:

1-2 sentence answers are more than sufficient. I sometimes zone out when a candidate talks more than that.

Complicated framework

Aim to have at maximum three metrics by which you judge your solution. Having a complicated prioritization framework can be confusing to interviewers. Also, it can be difficult to identify a clear winner when there's too many criterion. A Microsoft product manager said:

> *I do not understand why candidates think they need to choose some fancy weighted scoring or Kano models. It gets so complicated in the interview. Or some just ramble. Keep it simple.*

APPROACH

1. Ask interviewer "which one of these problems would you want to hear more about?" or "is there any specific problem/solution you'd like to hear more about?"
2. They are going to say, "you pick."
3. Pick a structure for prioritization. Keep it super simple, look below for sample prioritization frameworks.
4. Take 2–3 minutes to think through your answer and trade-offs (do not just immediately start talking).
5. State your chosen solution. About 70% of ideal answers had their top answer first.
6. Give 1–2 sentences comparing each idea against the criteria. Do not be too mechanical about this (e.g., this is high on this metric; this is low). About 80% of the ideal answers provided only 1–2 sentences for each comparison.
7. Optional: Instead of eliminating options completely, phrase solutions by timeline: What I am doing a) now, b) next, and c) later.
8. Reiterate the chosen option.

Picking prioritization frameworks

None of the ideal answers had a complicated framework, 100% of them used less than three metrics. Almost all ideal answers choose some version of "impact" vs "cost." They used different names:

- "benefit to user vs price"
- "value vs effort"

- "effective vs cheap"
- None called it "pros" and "cons" because that would be too general.

An Uber product manager explained the commonality:

> *When you are doing solution prioritization, "impact" should always be one of the metrics. You can name it whatever you want, but there should be a measure of how well you are solving the actual problem. If you have found the right problem, this should be the most import-ant metric in your entire prioritization metric. You know you have made a mistake when this metric is not guiding you to the best solu-tion. You most likely made a mistake in choosing the right problem. The other prioritization metrics can act as constraints to help you determine the best solution, and you should optimize for impact. For example, if you are solving a solution for the poor, even if you solve the problem effectively, cost would be the biggest constraint.*

Common phrases

- When phrasing solutions by timeline: "we can prioritize these solutions, but I also think that we can potentially layer them so we can go through them."
- "Picking this [solution] because company already has this advantage to double down on."
- [Feature] should be almost invisible, almost seamless.
- Design product that has no dead-ends, but instead have delightful experiences.

APPLYING TO EXAMPLE PROBLEM

> *"How would you improve Alexa to increase usage?", answered by Amazon principal product manager*

I want to prioritize these solutions by:

1. impact and
2. ease-of-implementation.

Of these, the second solution is the best. The first one will not solve the problem that much and the third problem, although would be very cool, would be very difficult to implement. Think the second solution can make the experience of shopping quite delightful if you do not have to go to an employee for every question.

WHAT WOWS INTERVIEWERS

Powerful product vision

Product vision is your opportunity to sell your solution to the interviewer and also allows you to signpost your work so far. Read the section on Formulating product vision later in this chapter to learn more. About 80% of ideal answers had a product vision and 100% of product managers said they found it very helpful when a candidate provided a product vision. A Coinbase product manager said:

> *Product vision is how I do my job. I need to sell my product managers, my engineering managers, my design managers on my product, and I need to be able to paint an inspiring and clear picture. I am obviously looking to see if the candidate can do that.*

Thoughtful UI

Designing a user interface and/or explaining the flow of the user experience is an important skill to demonstrate in the product management interview. To really differentiate yourself, it is valuable to design a particularly thoughtful user interface. As in, one that solves the high-level problem while also accommodating for minor pain points.

Interviewers thought only ~10% of candidates did a good job at this. Read the sections later on in this chapter on "Do's of UX" and "Do nots of UX" so that you can use some of these principles in the interview to design great user experiences. A Facebook product manager said:

*I remember one time the candidate was designing a Facebook prod-
uct to help immigrants/new-comers find doctors in a new area. They
had the sense to design the screens to be immediately localizable such
that they worked in both right to left and left to right languages. Since
we were designing for immigrants, that was exactly the design detail
I was looking to see.*

WHAT PUTS OFF INTERVIEWERS

Most candidates don't get to this part of the interview so interviewers didn't
provide enough data

- Not getting to this part of the interview
- Not considering the previous detail you spoke of

  *If you said you are designing for seniors, and you previously said
  we need to make it easy to use, when you start designing the phone
  screen, or web, or physical product, it'd be better if you at least made
  the buttons really big. It's the design detail that puts you over the
  top.—LinkedIn product manager*

APPROACH

- Summarize your design with a product vision (see Formulating product
  vision below)
- Delineate the flow for users
- Confirm with interviewer about flow
- (Optional) Write out/draw flow
- Draw some screens for the major parts of the flow on whiteboard or paper
  or digital whiteboard
- Before your interview, if you are using a digital whiteboard, keep exam-
  ple designs in the whiteboard that you can use during the interview (e.g.,
  pre-design some phone screens, web browser, and a simple flow diagram)

Formulating product vision

As a recap, product vision is your opportunity to sell your solution to the interviewer. It also allows you to signpost your work so far. **Craft a compelling**

vision very carefully as a good one seems to be very impressive to inter-viewers.

The ideal one sounds like a great marketing tagline that can be pasted on bill-boards and digital ads across the world. It will also be plastered on the wall of your engineer and design officers to (hopefully) inspire them. Create a vision that does two things:

1. Explains exactly what it does.
2. Captures why a user would want it.

Tips

- DON'T include the tech in your vision (e.g., machine learning, AR), as that only complicates the vision and is detail that is unnecessary to the user.
- Keep it as simple as possible, the shorter the better. Marketing taglines are not usually longer than seven words.
- Before you voice your answer, ensure that it is something that excites you. If it does not excite you, spend 30 more seconds and simplify it.
- Envision your product in 10 years!
- As much as possible, do not let current tech limit or color your vision (e.g., if you are making a garbage can that automatically sorts trash, do not let current vision capabilities limit you from pitching a grander product vi-sion around enabling circular economies).

Useful words

"personal assistant," "seamless service," "delightful," "seamless"

Examples

Here's examples of bad vs good product visions:

- "a closet that selects outfits for you based off your interest and availability" vs "a personal fashion assistant"
- "a VR app that allows you to interact with your friends real time while playing fun games that seamlessly removes any friction" vs "a digital play-ground that makes you forget you are not in real life"
- "a wearable that tracks your heart rate and shows you apps and other rele-vant info" vs "a watch that tracks your life, and time"

- "the fridge that tracks your normal level of food and orders groceries for you" vs "the fridge that seamlessly stocks itself"
- "an app that tracks your day to find where you waste your time to get you back on track" vs "a digital warden"
- "an app that connects you with potential roommates and a great apartment based off advanced machine learning" vs "a service that pairs you with lifelong friends and a great home"
- "a social network for professionals" vs "an app that creates economic opportunity for every member of the global workforce by connecting professionals"

Do's of UX Design

There are various principles of UI/UX Design that people spend years mastering. Here are the most important points that product managers use regularly when designing UI/UX. Understand them and remember to use them or at least note them during the interview so that the interviewer knows you are familiar with them.

Remember to enhance the user's image of themselves. The best way to turn a user into an advocate is to enhance the user in their context. E.g.: Instead of "I have a good camera," let the product make the user feel "I am a good photographer!" Below are UX principles to help accomplish that.

- **Reduce cognitive load** inherent in using your product. Cognitive load is anything that the user must learn or keep constantly in mind to use your product.
- **Device agnostic UI.** Gone are the days of 'mobile-friendly' websites. In the rapidly expanding design business, it is quintessential to be *Device Agnostic.* It is no longer going to be a choice for businesses to design the UX for single platforms. Responsive UX is inevitable for businesses that want to succeed in the digital experiences race. The aim for UX Design in 2019 should be to deliver a seamless experience irrespective of the device it is being delivered for.
- **Make it easier to focus.** The digital age has a lot to offer to the users and the digital platform's creators often tend to incorporate TOO much information and points of attraction on a single screen. Contrary to that, design a screen that serves only one problem statement. Including more features without cluttering the viability is optimum. Design screens that your users can clearly figure out the flow on the app/website with a single point of focus.

- **Reduce the number of choices** to be made by keeping it simple. Being minimalistic is not a niche design language anymore. It is a mainstream adopted format. Look at Chromecast, Alexa, iPhone, Zoom, etc. They are all extremely simple products. A deadly misconception that employing a greater number of features can improve sales. Designers are often forced to add features even if the design is already over-loaded!! This can be somewhat overwhelming for new/ first-time users. For a design to be successful, try to have a focused limited set of features which are solving your major problem statement. Therefore, it is vital to prioritize what is important.
- **Reduce the steps.** This can be in contradiction to Keep it simple because it can be difficult to reduce the number of steps while removing most buttons. However, it is important to reduce the steps to the most popular/ used buttons. For example, rather than having a radio with one button for everything, having multiple, clearly labelled buttons is more helpful.

Do nots of UX Design

Do not worry about quick content loading, legible typefaces, simple and minimalistic designs, theme-based color palettes, and some other minor features to add are points every UX Designer takes care of these days.

- **Asking authorization permission right at the start.** Quite often as we just launch a just-downloaded app, there's a shower of app permissions (e.g., "Allow app X to use your location?"). Unless we have used the app and become well-aware of the app environment, how do you give the permissions? This is sure to make the users hostile. Users often deny such permission requests because, at the very beginning, the users do not have any context to decide. They do not know why your app needs those permissions. To mitigate such behavior, it is better to ask for permissions in context and communicate the value the access will provide. Users are more likely to grant permissions if asked during a relevant task. Request permissions at launch only when it is necessary for the core app UX.
- **Do not let the user hit a dead-end. Always redirect or remove dead-ends.** UX is all about user flow, their interactions with every individual screen. A dead-end on the app/website is the biggest turn-off for a user. Dead-ends act as blockers for user flow: they create confusion and lead to additional, often unnecessary actions. Remove the dead-end option completely or redirect them immediately to a new page with a banner indicating that their previous action did not work.

- **Avoid using jargon while keeping language precise.** It is all about making the users comfortable in their own skin. Unnecessary use of jargon to make it look ***oh-so-fancy*** can lead to the user not understanding what the app is trying to convey. The prime goal: the user must be comfortable with the language and the words used on the screen. The app must have only standard words that do not increase the cognitive load for the user. E.g., "Your user named and/or password do not match" is better than "You cannot login to the application."
- **Personalize content; never personalize UI or actions**, especially *personalized gestures* as a primary way of interacting with the app. This limits the user interaction with the app. Sometimes these gestures can be the supporting mechanism for the mobile app. However, it is best to avoid too many gestures and stick to the standard ones, as standardization is the key to a good UX of the app. The mobile user needs to see standard symbols and controls for the common actions to be able to recognize them easily.

APPLYING TO EXAMPLE PROBLEM

"How would you improve Alexa to increase usage?," answered by Amazon principal product manager

So, what I am building here is a "delightful store assistant."

Each retail store would have a different strategy for placement so I am going to spend time designing the actual button and flow that would activate Alexa.

I am envisioning a large circular speaker that can be attached to a wall that says "Push for Alexa" on the top surface. The customer will be able to push in the button and Alexa will activate asking "How can I help you find what you need today?"

In case Alexa cannot answer the question, then it can ping an associate with its location for more help.

Ideal Answers: Product Design

4

Improve the Experience in Finding a Place to Rent

Asked and answered by Uber Group product manager

WHAT INTERVIEWER LOOKS FOR

- *"I actually love this problem because it forces the candidate to focus on so many different aspects of the user journey and the different stakeholders involved."*
- *"I want to make sure they can design a solution that works in the marketplace. In this case, don't need to come up with something crazy, just work to solve the actual problem—it's a difficult problem."*

COMMON MISTAKES

- *"There is actually a common problem whenever I give this question. People completely miss the landlord's portion, which is a key part of this problem, it becomes a lot more interesting when you start to consider landlord's problem and renter's problems.*
- *Honestly, the user brainstorm part does not super matter either, people spend a lot of time thinking they have to come up with the fanciest user segmentation or some cool user. While that would be impressive, it is more important that you follow a linear approach in picking your users, so that you pick something that's mostly logical."*

ANSWER

This answer contains: Stakeholders > Users > User selection > User problem > Problem prioritization > Solutions > Solution prioritization > Conclusion

Stakeholders

At a high level, there's too big buckets.

- Renters
- Landlords

Overall, will pick to solve the problem for renters as I'm a bit more familiar with their problems.

Users

There are four main user groups that I want to target:

- Immigrants (from other countries)
- Graduates
- Old families
- Young families

User selection

I'm going to prioritize these users by:

- Frequency of movement
- Knowledge of renting space (e.g., how lost are they?)
- Ability

Applying the criteria to each user:

- Young families: Interesting but probably have sufficient knowledge, especially in the local area
- New grads is the second biggest opportunity: they're going to move a couple of times and they repeat
- Immigrant families are biggest opportunity: they're going to move, as they find jobs, schools and they have no knowledge of the area

So, I'm going to pick immigrant families as the best user group to solve for.

User problem

Overall, renters care about

- Price
- Trust
- Location

Immigrant families in particular care about:

- Good schools
- Similar immigrant background
- Immigrant ratings (potentially)
- Landlord with similar immigrant background (potentially)

I'm going to do the user journey that immigrant families follow:

- Have need to rent house
- Get information for best cities to move to in country
- Get information on best neighborhoods in city for immigrant community, schools, etc.
- Go online (e.g., Craiglists) to search for rental homes
- Pick between homes, potentially even by asking friends to help determine best home or asking friend to check home (if have one in city)
- Understand lease terms
- Sign deal

Problem prioritization

Biggest pain point seems to be around picking neighborhoods in which immigrant families could integrate into with good schools.

Solutions

- Rental site that can filter by immigrant background and see what others in your community have bought
- Culture-specific service that checks house and communicates to buyer in their language (e.g., previous Indian immigrant checking out home for next Indian immigrant)
- VR that allows you to check out a home

Solution prioritization

- Prioritizing by impact and effort
- Service that checks out house is the best idea by those standards, solves the problem for the immigrant as they trust previous immigrants and the system and while it will take effort to recruit previous buyers, hopefully it will create a network
- VR to check out doesn't solve the problem effectively
- Rental site that allows you see what other immigrants have bought is very helpful but would be too difficult to build.

Conclusion

Create a network service to have previous immigrants check out homes on behalf of new immigrants for a fee or provide general advice.

MY THOUGHTS

For the solution, liked that she inserted something crazy/creative in there, even if she didn't pick it. Also, she didn't discuss every single option and debate every single reasoning. She made a decision and moved on.

How Would You Improve Alexa to Increase Usage?

Asked and answered by an Amazon principal product manager

WHAT INTERVIEWER LOOKS FOR

> *"I really like this question because it is actually quite difficult to answer. Alexa already does so much and is quite versatile. You must be able to correctly identify the gaps in their product according to each user. You need deep user empathy but also the ability to understand strategy. I'll provide my ideal answer to this question. If someone gave me this answer, they'd be a strong hire."*

COMMON MISTAKES

> *"The problem that most candidates run into when facing this question is that they focus on the miniature changes. Who cares about adding a cooking flow to Alexa? You think that's going to double usage or wow anybody? Yet 90% of the candidates end up proposing that."—Amazon principal product manager*

ANSWER

Goal

We want to increase usage of Alexa and the orders of products and services associated with Alexa (e.g., Echo).

User selection

Okay, I would like to start by talking about the types of users that are likely to buy voice-controlled assistant devices like the Amazon Echo, who they are and what things they may want to do that the current Amazon Echo product does not support. After brainstorming on some use cases related to voice-controlled assistants, I will select the ones that I think would help achieve the goals if backed by a new feature.

The main current types of users of Alexa are:

- Families that are technology savvy and have mid- to high disposable incomes to buy non-essential electronic devices.
- Elderly parents of potential buyers (kids would be the buyers)
- Single individuals

Want to expand and think of new users:

- Retail stores
- Offices

Okay, I would like to take a minute to brainstorm possible use cases that have not been addressed by Amazon Echo for these three users yet.

Families:

- Do not have time to plan their meals, such as deciding what to cook, which ingredients to buy, and how to cook the meal.
- Assistance in choosing a recipe, buying ingredients, and step-by-step instructions on how to cook would save them time.
- Finding folks to service home
- Children learning a new language or skill.

Elderly:

- Remembering which medication to take, at what times, and in which order to take them
- Forgetting key information, such as family information or situational awareness. For example, forgetting that you have two sons and they're visiting today.

Single individual:

- Public speaking coaching is something many professionals are interested in
- Having a personal trainer for exercising
- Learning how to play an instrument. Could correct your wrong tones and allows you to be handsfree.

Retail stores:

- Service customers immediately
- Manage inventory seamlessly
- Handle employee knowledge and concerns.

Office workplace:

- Order food for the workplace
- Order requirements for the office (e.g., chair, monitor).

User prioritization

If our goal is to increase Amazon overall revenue and increase Alexa footprint, I want to target two things in my prioritization:

1.	whitespace (most opportunity for Amazon to create new use cases) and
2.	largest user category.

Based on these two factors, I think retail stores are the most interesting users/ buyers in this scenario based on these two prioritization criteria.

We could have thousands of users using the retail store solutions even with only one buyer (one retail store) on a daily basis. We also haven't really played in the business space before, so it has the most whitespace for new solutions.

A segment of the other users are already using Alexa. While we can think of some killer-use cases for them, I don't know if we'll drastically increase daily users, as we could with the business option.

Problem-brainstorming

The problems would have to be centered around conversation, so between the customer and the employee or the employee and the customer.

- Fulfilling customer service requests
- Answering customer questions in-store
- Facilitating curbside pickup scenarios (e.g., instead of ordering ahead, can you order takeout through Amazon Echo in a drive-through?)
- Handling employee requests for time-off or questions about inventory

Problem prioritization

Of all these use cases, I would prioritize the ones that are more likely to help achieve the goals stated earlier: to increase purchases of the Echo and increase purchases of products and services from other Amazon businesses. The use cases that would be aligned with these goals would be those that are important to the user and frequent enough for the user to want to buy the Amazon Echo. Ideally, they should also lead to the frequent purchase of products and services from Amazon.

Therefore my criteria for prioritizing problems is:

1.	whether it is an important use case
2.	whether it can be reasonably done by Alexa.

Based on these, I think answering customer service questions in-store would be the best problem to focus on. We can solve it with Alexa and it is an extremely important problem for retailers and for users.

Solutions

There are a couple of ways to solve this problem:

1. Alexa integrated into the company mobile app so that they can ask questions through there
2. Buttons around the store that customers can press to ask Alexa questions
3. Alexa service that you can just ask for all your orders and it instructs an employee to retrieve it.

Solution prioritization

I want to prioritize these solutions by:

1. impact and
2. ease-of-implementation.

Of these, the second solution is the best. The first one won't solve the problem that much and the third problem, although would be very cool, would be very difficult to implement. Think the second solution can make the experience of shopping quite delightful if you don't have to go to an employee for every question.

Solution design

Each retail store would have a different strategy for placement so I'm going to spend time designing the actual button that would activate Alexa.

I'm envisioning a large circular speaker that can be attached to a wall that says "Push for Alexa" on the top surface. The customer will be able to push in the button and Alexa will activate asking "How can I help you find what you need today?".

In case Alexa can't answer the question, then it can ping an associate with its location for more help.

Summary of risks

In summary, I have explored use cases that the Amazon Echo has not yet addressed. I think we should explore building out Alexa for Business so that customers can get answers immediately to their questions.

There's a couple of risks for which I've laid out the mitigation plan:

- Businesses don't want to brand their buttons with "Alexa" -> can offer to change the button title
- Alexa won't answer the questions accurately -> ensure that we build APIs that integrate into their ERP tool and test before release
- Businesses don't want to buy from Amazon -> ensure that we won't release any data back to Amazon or use any information.

MY THOUGHTS

I really liked that she chose businesses because that is a whitespace and creates a lot of opportunity for good, creative ideas rather than just something slightly incremental, like a speech coach or something. There's other options if she'd chosen the individual/family personas: cooking instructions, memory aids, medication reminders, etc. but none of them would have significantly increased Alexa usage. (Think, would cooking instructions triple the usage? Definitely not.) Also loved the use of 'delightful', using these key phrases helps to convince the interviewer that your work is impressive.

Design a Better Backpack

Asked and answered by Facebook Product Manager

WHAT INTERVIEWER LOOKS FOR

Most people in this scenario go straight to the typical student scenario. It is important to list users and show empathy. The goal setting doesn't matter here as much, candidates don't need to spend too much time on it as the problem is to goal is given in the problem

COMMON MISTAKES

Most candidates always resort to a tech solution, and it's always the same stuff: charger in backpack, a connected backpack, etc. Whenever I see those questions, it takes an effort for me to not roll my eyes. At that point, unless they do really well on another aspect, it's just a no for me. Think of anything that is even reasonably creative and as long as you follow a thoughtful process, it's a much better answer.

ANSWER

Some clarifying questions:

Is there a business objective to increase revenue or focus on a target user base that you for this new product? Do you already have a keyboard out in the market, and are focusing on a niche market now? Or are we trying to enter a market with a new product?

[Interviewer] : We already have a generic keyboard, but want to focus on increasing sales.

I'm going to broaden the scenario a bit to not just include backpacks but also anything that holds useful things for somebody between two places that's not a suitcase.

Interviewer: "Why?"

This will allow me to broaden the scope to focus on interesting problems and solutions. If I just focus on backpacks, I'm constraining myself to a type of solution without identifying the problem.

Interviewer: "Sure"

User identification:

Various people use backpacks. The main two buckets of people I'm thinking of are:

- students
- office workers
- travellers
  - o Businesspeople
  - o Travellers—intense
  - o Students
  - o Others—janitors
  - o Small backpack

They each have different uses they want out of their "backpacks". Students want something that's (in order):

1. cheap
2. large
3. potentially cheek.

Office workers want:

1. good looking
2. comfortable
3. compact.

Backpackers want:

1. large
2. light
3. durable.

User prioritization:

In terms of which user to pick to go forward with it, I'm really excited about the office worker. If I look at their needs, I really don't think that's solved today. There's plenty of backpacks for students and for backpackers that are large, cheap, and durable. However, none of them really hit the spot for office workers.

- Prioritization
  - o   Biggest problem with holding things
  - o   Business people—60%
  - o   Girls—50%

So I'm going to proceed with office workers.

- Pick businesspeople: hold
  - o   Laptop
  - o   Charger
  - o   Lunch
  - o   Papers
  - o   Others

Pain points

I covered the pain points earlier, but I think they're still a bit too high level. Hard to design a product knowing all users want is something that's fancy and compact—hundreds of companies are trying and failing to do that today. To dig in deeper, I want to focus on a category of office workers that I think is potentially feeling this pain the most: the young female.

They have to choose between professional but cool, compact but large enough for their day, and functional but accessible. Handbags are too small or not that functional. Normal backpacks are not professional enough and don't look mature. Laptop bags could work but don't look good. Essentially, we need a sleek backpack built for office women. Okay, so for females, we need something that:

- looks good
- is small but can contain a laptop
- is built for women (e.g., can contain key items for the day, potentially even a separate sanitary pad holder)
- picking backpack
  - o   looks
  - o   ergonomics—heavy
  - o   price
  - o   accessibility
- pain points—looks nice
  - o   briefcases
    - ▪   look nice
    - ▪   but they're heavy to carry

- o backpacks
    - multiple folds
    - **multiple zippers**
    - get dirty
    - arm straps not great because it could affect your dress or your suit
  - o satchel
- what are they using instead of backpacks
- what are great things about briefcase
- how can we make great things about briefcase, remove things from brief-case into customer group

Solution

- solutions—outside look
  - o sleek backpack with multiple folds—same nisite but nice outside
  - o what if zippers were on onsite
  - o backpack that becomes briefcase

MY THOUGHTS

The goal-setting does not matter here as much, I liked that we didn't spend too much time on it. Almost all product managers follow a strict structure for prioritization. They don't just start speaking about what is good vs bad, but compare each user or solution to a strict metric. While all of them asked questions, none of them asked what next to do, but were proactive in their direction and checked to make sure that we were on time. Instead of "should I do solutions next?," they all opted for "I'm going to dive into solutions next since we have 5 minutes left, does that make sense?"

Really like that we expanded beyond just backpacks to the broader problem of "holding things." Obviously, need to confirm that change with the interviewer, but that allowed us to come up with more creative solutions and not fall into the 'connected backpack' problem.

WHAT INTERVIEWER LOOKS FOR

"I really like this question because it is so simple, it pushes the candidate to be creative. Use cases are at the heart of this question. You have to make assumptions fast to progress through the case."

ANSWER

I would like to start by identifying who the customers are, what their pain points are, then I will brainstorm ideas for design and monetization for the stand that address the customer's needs.

User

- All kinds of people eat ice cream: friends, families, single people of all ages, and tourists.

Let me provide an overview of each user and their overall habits.

- Friends: Friends visit the park to play team sports or relax together on the grass. They may want an ice cream if a stand is nearby. Usually, one or two friends will get ice cream for the group.
- Families: Parents will most likely walk to the ice-cream stand with their children. Waiting to order with kids can be stressful for parents since they have to supervise.
- Single people: Individuals may go to the park to relax or read a book. They may have found a terrific spot and do not want to give it up. If they want to get ice cream, a pain point for them is leaving their spot to get an ice cream.
- Tourists: If pressed for time and the line is long, they may not want to wait to buy an ice cream.

General pain points

In general, I think most people would like the following ice-cream stand experiences to be better:

- Most people would prefer to have the ice cream come to them.
- In most cases, people want their ice-cream fast.
- Before ordering, most people want to know what they look like and how they taste.
- Individuals making group orders would like to help carry the ice creams back to their friends or family.
- A simpler way to pay when buying for a group.

Looks like these problems cut across all demographics so I won't focus on a single user, but will try to tackle all of them.

Solutions

Here are some ideas:

- Ordering ice cream as a delivery: Instead of people coming to the ice-cream stand, we can use tricycles
- Ice cream as a buffet
- Entertainment-style performances to get people to come watch performances and buy ice cream
- Ice-cream vending machines
- Boat style ice-cream tasting section.

Solution Prioritization

I will evaluate each idea on impact vs. cost.

Looking at all the options, the best ideas are the Entertainment and Ice cream for delivery ideas. Both have high impact scores, with the delivery idea just a bit higher than the entertainment idea. But the entertainment idea costs less.

The entertainment idea seems less risky to me. It can be cut anytime but the delivery idea, however, requires capital investment. So, I will choose the entertainment idea, because it costs less and carries less risk.

Solution design

The entertainment idea provides the fun customers come to buy ice cream for. Also, I think streamlining the ordering and payment process for ice cream would add value to my customers and increase monetization. Here are some parts of the flow

- A small stage in the ice cream shop for local performers to come to work for tips
- An hourly lottery to win free ice cream: This would appeal to customers' expectations of having fun at the park. Customers can sign up for the lottery through an app.

Summary and risks

To summarize, after analyzing scenarios at the park in which people find themselves wanting ice cream, I synthesized a list of common customer needs. I proposed several ice-cream stand ideas to address these needs and chose the best one based on impact vs. cost and level of financial risk. The best idea was the entertainment addition to the ice-cream stand. I also recommended streamlining the ordering, payment, and delivery of our ice cream via a mobile app.

MY THOUGHTS

This is not a great answer. I think it is actually a bit silly to have focused on all the users in this case. The solutions we investigated weren't even related to the user brainstorming that we did. This solution missed a couple of key parts:

- User prioritization
- User pain point/flow identification
- Pain point prioritization

If the answer had these parts, we could have gotten to a much more clear and delightful solution. For example, let's investigate another alternative:

- User: let's pick young adults as they have disposable income and are not too worried about unhealthy impact, but are more worried about convenience, taste, and shareable content.

- Major problem: Young adults are the largest demographic of food delivery services. If you've ever ordered ice cream through a delivery service, it is hard for ice cream to get delivered through food delivery services (it melts, can get mushed, often comes in lame packaging).
- Solution: create delightful packaging for ice cream that keeps the ice-cream cone safe and when opened, shoots confetti in the air. This creates shareable content and is very convenient.

Personally, I would buy the confetti ice cream. And it's a lot more interesting and compelling problem. And it's a lot more compelling to the interviewer that you understand your user.

Not spending enough time on the user and the pain point results in a solution that doesn't solve a compelling problem.

Advice for Video Interviews

Video interviews were quite common before the pandemic and will be common for the next few years, at least. Here are three suggestions to ensure you put your best foot forward:

1. OPTIMIZE YOUR BACKGROUND AND LIGHTING

- **Most important: Use the rule of thirds to frame your face.** This rule of thumb from photography says that you should divide a picture in thirds horizontally and vertically, creating a sort of tic-tac-toe grid, and then put the most interesting things along those lines or at the intersections.
- **Make sure light shines on the front of your face** instead of being on top of you or behind you. Ring lights, a favorite of influencers everywhere, are great for this.
- **Use a unique background,** but do not worry about it too much.

2. ENGAGE YOUR INTERVIEWER ACTIVELY

- **Act natural**, do not worry about having to investigate the webcam or the screen. You do not even need to alternate. Just do not obsess over how you look, that is distracting you for no reason!

- **Check in and signpost more often.** In an in-person interview, you can usually read the interviewer's body language to figure out if they are confused or think you are going down the wrong path. It's much harder to read this on a video call. So, instead, use phrases like, "Does that make sense?" or "Sound good?" regularly. This gives you more opportunities to course-correct and avoid veering into rabbit holes. In-person, you'd usually write down your steps on the whiteboard (define the problem, ask clarifying questions, break the problem into pieces, etc.) and gesture to them as you complete each step. Even with a digital whiteboard, gesturing is harder on a video call, so be extra verbose and say when you are starting and ending each step. This will help your interviewer understand your process and make you come across as a more methodical, organized person.

- **Do not talk all the time!** Pause, take a lot of time, enumerate your points, and be super clear. Because the interviewer is more likely to get distracted in front of the computer, make sure that you do not ramble. It's much easier to ignore you and stare at the screen if you are droning. If you engage them with high-value content, they are less likely to start ignoring you.

- **Be happy!** Tech workers spend all day on boring, draining Zoom calls. Make your interview the highlight of their day—show how happy you are to be there, throw some fun ideas into your interview answers, and ask for their opinion (people love sharing their opinions). Most importantly, make sure you smile and bring the energy!

3. USE A DIGITAL DOC AND DIGITAL WHITEBOARD

- **Create a Google Doc** and share with the interviewer. It's even better if you send them a link so they can interact with your designs in real time.

- **Use Google Jamboard** and send the interviewer a link or share your screen.

- **Do not use a handheld whiteboard** and hold it up to the camera every so often. The pacing will get weird, since you cannot draw and show the interviewer the whiteboard at the same time, and the interviewer won't be able to see much detail.